The New INTERNATIONAL BESTSELLER
Over One Million Copies Sold i...

The
META
SECRET
is
THE NEXT LEVEL

THE LAW OF ATTRACTION IS ONE OF SEVEN ANCIENT PRINCIPLES
HERE ARE THE OTHER SIX.

MEL GILL

II

"The principles of Truth
are Seven;
he who knows these understandingly,
possesses the magic key
before whose touch
all the doors
of the temple of Solomon
fly open."

The Kybalion

For

Mamaji, Papaji and Phupi

Without you

These pages would have been empty

The Meta Secret™

is
The Next Level

Mel Gill

PANDORA
PUBLISHING HOUSE

First published in Chicago & Singapore, 2010
by Pandora Publishing House
A division of
DMG Capital Corporation, BVI

www.PandoraPublishing.com

Copyright © 2010, 2011, 2012 by DMG Capital Corporation,

This book is copyrighted,
Apart from fair dealing for the purpose of private study, research, criticism or preview, as permitted under the Copyright Act, no part may be reproduced by any process without written permission. All Inquiries, including Bulk Discounts should be addressed to the publisher.

Pandora Publishing House, Chicago
205 East Butterfield Road
Suite 138
Elmhurst, IL 60126

E-mail: enquiries@pandorapublishing.com
drmelgill@pandorapublishing.com

Tel: (630) 908 2948 (Chicago)
(914) 230 4933 (New York)

ISBN 978 - 147 - 91 - 3491 - 5

GILL, MEL.
THE META SECRET - DMG Capital Corporation 2012.
204 p.
1. Thought and Thinking. 2. Psychology, Applied. I. Title.
153.42

The publisher and author expressly disclaim liability to any person for the consequences of anything done or omitted to be done by such person in reliance, whether in whole or in part upon any part of the contents of this publication.

Table of Contents

ACKNOWLEDGEMENTS — pg X
PREFACE - Joe Vitale — pg XII
FOREWORD - Jack Canfield — pg XIV
INTRODUCTION — pg XVII

PART ONE

Chapter 1 - The Day the World Changed — pg 2
Chapter 2 - Anything Is Possible — pg 18
Chapter 3 - What Goes Around, Comes Around — pg 34
Chapter 4 - Good Vibrations — pg 49
Chapter 5 - Everything Has An Opposite — pg 60
Chapter 6 - Go with the Flow — pg 70
Chapter 7 - To Everything There Is A Season — pg 82
Chapter 8 - Nothing Happens By Chance — pg 92

PART TWO

Chapter 9 - The Simplicity of Synchronicity — pg 107
Chapter 10 - Practicing Wealth — pg 117
Chapter 11 - Energizing Health — pg 131
Chapter 12 - Living Love — pg 147
Chapter 13 - Finding True Happiness — pg 166
Chapter 14 - The Best Days of Our Lives — pg 189

META SECRET

This book is dedicated to

that part of you

which knows that

all

men and women

are

brothers and sisters

connected

by dreams, hopes, love and desires

and that

no matter what

we achieve, accomplish or gain in this life

we leave it all behind

as trail markers for

fellow pilgrims on the journey

home.

Acknowledgements

To my children Luc and Aurora, who are my raison d'être and the real inspiration for everything I am today. I love you both for being patient with me and for allowing the freedom to make so many mistakes as I try to be the father you would like to "hang out" with.

To Bob Proctor, Joel Roberts, Jack Canfield, Dr. Joe Vitale, Dr. Masaru Emoto, Eli Davidson, David Riklan, T. Harv Eker, Dan Poynter, Jay Abraham, Arthur Carmazzi, W. Mitchell and Greg Heart who made this Movie possible by their generous and kind contributions to the Collective Wisdom of our Planet.

To my sister Indra who has been my most patient and constructive critic in helping me edit this book.

To Graham Smith and Doris Tan-Smith whose friendship and encouragement over the last fourteen years has nourished me and whose belief in me has never waivered in the years leading to The Meta Project. When everybody left me with nothing, you still stood by, gave me Everything….Thank you for pushing me 'inside' and out to finish this project.

To Teresa Hsu and Sharana Rao who are the true purveyors of The Meta Secret and whose legacy is in every word I write and teach. To Alison, Lauren, Emma, Kayla and Richard Humphries whose tireless feedback helped to shape the ideas that gave this book form.

To Richard Elep who did everything 'behind the scenes' from acting, to doing the accounts and my bills, to recruiting, to translating and to taking care of catering needs in making the Meta Secret a reality.

To Nora for your love, support and protection; even when you were angry with me you protected me from people who had evil intentions....I will always remember that. To Ms Chan for the translations from Japanese to English and for the many rides and meals you generously offered to "my crew" and I. To Jenny for the typing and filing of notes and scripts that kept me sane.

To Chris Lee, Eve and Yvonne, remember when I dreamed up this idea? You were there and Eve's words still echo in my brain. She is the real reason I decided one day that Anything is Possible. To Dilip Mukerjea who gave me much feedback and valuable insights that made this writing better. To Anitha & Shan who are the reason why this Meta Secret project began three years ago.

To the other Teachers of the Meta Secret who were not included here but to whom I owe a great debt of Gratitude; The Dalai Lama, Umesh Nandwani, Karl Moore, Christina Chia, Caroline, Ajahn Brahm, Kaliswari, Debra Thompson, Matt Bacak, Ewen Chia, Fabian Lim, Judith Williamson, Swami Rukumani, Thubten Chodron, Vickas Malkani, Wendy Quek and William Quek and finally, to the many who made it a smoother road to get here; Karen Gerberg, Kaz Cai, Ellen Feinberg, Axel Chan, Devi Haridas, Douglas Yeager, Norma Jean Wright, Diana Chan, Ye Pan and all my thousands of students who are also my teachers……..thank you all for being you!!!

Preface by Joe Vitale

When I was on Fox & Friends national television show in 2009, the host asked me what my doctorate degrees were in. I said I had one in marketing and one in metaphysical science.

"What's metaphysical science?" he asked.

I only had a moment to think of the best way to answer him. I knew whatever I said would confuse him. As a television journalist, he's used to talking about concrete reality, not thoughts, feelings, esoteric philosophy, mind power or much else. Yet I had to tell him the truth to maintain my own integrity.

"It's the study of the invisible," I replied.
He stared at me.
He admitted he had never heard of such a thing.

Of course he hadn't. Most people haven't. And that explains why most people struggle through life. They are giving all their attention to the physical, and almost none to the metaphysical. Yet it's in the latter where the real power and true magic resides. Swim there and you can make your life one of joy and miracles. Fortunately for us my dear friend Mel Gill has provided the tools you need to reach and play in the metaphysical arena. It's all in this book. It's the companion to his movie, and both are designed to take you deeper into life than you might ever have expected possible.

But like the reporter who didn't know there was a "Study of the Invisible," most people don't know that there is a META SECRET. But remember, most people (as Thoreau observed) are leading lives of quiet desperation. Most people don't know there's a way out that is easily accessible to everyone. And most people don't know that the way out is to go in. And that the way past our problems and trials and tribulations is to go through them. What makes the journey easier sometimes is a Guide. Mel has been that Guide for me and many others. This book is a great Tool-kit filled with the knowledge you need to do exactly that, get through Life using powerful Metaphysical concepts and by doing so, you will emerge with more Laughter, more Love and more Wealth than you dreamed possible!

Anything you want to change has to be changed on the inside first. As I once told an audience, trying to change the outer is like trying to put make-up on your mirror or even trying to shave your mirror! You don't want to clean up the mirror, you want to clean up you.

This Amazing book distilled from the Wisdom and Genius of my friend Mel Gill, tells you how to take care of yourself from the inside out. It's practical, hypnotic, inspiring and packed with mystical yet practical wisdom. His own story is riveting. It will nail you to the page. His personal insights are nuggets of wisdom you can instantly apply in your life. This book is the Secret Wisdom of the Universe in print for the first time in Centuries!

Said more accurately, it's the Meta-Secret of the Universe. When you're ready to discover the META SECRET of your life, just turn the page...

Joe Vitale
Metaphysician

Foreword by Jack Canfield

When I was first sent this book to read, I recognized its title from the movie by the same name that my friend Mel Gill had shot last year with me, Bob Proctor, Joe Vitale, Charlie "Tremendous" Jones, Dr. Masaru Emoto, and several other eminent pioneers in the field of human development. In the movie we discussed the Meta concepts around the Law of Attraction and one's ability to manifest a life filled with Wealth, Love, Health and Happiness. I remembered our conversations on the balcony just outside the hotel room in Santa Barbara and how Mel, with humor and passion began to narrate the story of his life and how he came to the point of creating "The Meta Secret."

At that point in time this book was just a concept, and its contents were to include the "Hidden" Laws that work in concert with the Laws of Attraction. Mel had outlined the Seven Laws of Hermes Trismegistus, "the messenger of the gods," and how to apply them to specific events or situations in our lives. He talked about the need to heighten our awareness and awaken to our higher potentials and to our true authentic selves. He said that life was simply a dance of energy and emotions linked to the highest good that we are able to express through love and kindness. Our conversation centered on his pivotal concept that we had to take responsibility for our own emotional states, and that our happiness did not depend on what others did or said, but was entirely dependent on our connectedness to "Source" and the radiant presence that streams through us with pure positive energy and possibilities. It is this connection to Source energy that allows us to rise beyond limitations or conditions and gifts us with freedom, power, goodness, love, and a sense of purpose and direction so that nothing can stop us from achieving any goal or reaching any destination. And it is on that path that we discover the "Meta Secret" to everything we have ever truly needed to know. And as a result our days are then filled with an incredible sense of joy and fun, and as far as we are concerned, "All is well."

The Seven Hermetic Laws are as complex to explain as they are even more complex to illustrate. Yet in this book, Mel has simplified them and explained them so elegantly that one begins to wonder why they were so hard to understand in the first place.

There is the immutable Law of Correspondence, The Law of Mentalism, The Law of Polarity, The Law of Cause and Effect, The Law of Gender, The Law of Vibration and The Law of Rhythm. All of these Laws combine in various ways and in different degrees to give us what we inevitably experience as The Law of Attraction. A thorough understanding of the Principles contained within these pages will give you a sense of calm and a peace of mind that will follow you into any experience life unfolds for you. You do not have to aspire to higher consciousness nor be filled with compassion and faith to understand that ALL things are available to you now and that you can create the Life you truly desire. All you need are the set of tools and the philosophies contained in The Meta Secret, and you can unlock the gates to the Temple of Solomon wherein lie great treasures and wisdom.

There have been many sages throughout the years that have written about these Seven Hermetic Laws in works like The Kybalion and The Emerald Tablet, but in this day and age, we are fortunate to have a person like Mel Gill, who not only truly understands these Principles, but teaches them as part of his interaction with everyone he meets. He is an Urban Sage dispensing wisdom through his seminars, workshops and radio show, and now he has distilled all that into the book you hold in your hands. As Mel would tell you, it is not an accident that you are now reading this book. It was meant to be; it is your Destiny.

I was inspired by Mel's aura of calm and serenity when I first met him, and today I feel truly blessed to count him as a dear friend. A wise teacher once told me that we should be a teacher to those below us, a fellow traveler to those on the same level, and a student to those above us. Wisely I have chosen to be one of Mel's students and I am always learning something new from him every time we are together!

This book that you hold in your hands is an amazing true story of a young man who sets out on a journey of discovery, and through much adversity and pain discovers the real Secrets of the Universe. From the unfortunate accident on the mountain top where he lost his arm, to the operating room where he went through a "Near-Death Experience," he has demonstrated great courage and resolve with a singular focus…..to remember the lessons he learned from the Light and to share these lessons with the world.

Mel and I share a mutual friend in Charlie "Tremendous" Jones, who unfortunately died of cancer during the making of "The Meta Secret" movie, and I can't help but wonder if Charlie might not echo my sentiments exactly when I say that this book is truly TREMENDOUS !!!

I know that you will benefit from reading this book as much as I have!

From my heart to yours,

Jack Canfield

Introduction

It was a dark night on December 19th 1976 when the world changed for me. It was the day I died!

I was dead for 19 minutes, by all counts I should not be alive today. Should not be able to talk let alone walk. But I survived a serious fall, and an operation that followed in which my left arm was amputated from above the elbow. They said it was to fight the gas gangrene which now had spread through my whole body. I literally felt my organs begin to shut down one by one, like someone turning off the lights in the room. First my kidneys, my liver, my heart then my lungs gave way. In that instant I was separated from my body and took a journey to a place I am still only now, remembering bit by bit.

The Lessons I was taught were profound and what for me seemed like days happened in the flash of 19 minutes. These lessons became conscious knowing as the years passed and I was left with certain "gifts" that only my closest friends are privy to. Over the years I became a Motivational Speaker and a Therapist.

I even had a Radio Show for 7 years. It ran for 3 hours a day 5 days a week and I found myself "dispensing" the wisdom that I was taught in that Realm of Masters (My term for it because of the many 'masters' I became student to). Through it all, living an absolutely "normal" life from Seattle to New York to now having my home in Chicago and offices in the Far East, I did not feel any different from my siblings or my friends. But there was a 'distance', a nagging feeling that I did not belong……to any place.

Every encounter, every emotion was lived as if it was someone else living it. A wonderful consolidation took place in the Far East in 1999 where all my polarities spontaneously collapsed….became one.

No more good or bad, or up and down, hot or cold, near or far, in or out, east or west, male or female, sad or happy…….more than five hundred polarities were collapsing and becoming one and I was no longer the "I" that I knew. I became something else. No longer did I see friend or enemy, just brothers and sisters on a vast journey guided by an unknowable force beyond description….beyond words. I kept "remembering" scrolls and tablets and books that were "living". I mean, the books would change words as you held them and all that I have known continues to change and evolve even after the fact!

I shared what I could muster into recognizable language and kept silent about the rest. It was wiser to simply say "I don't know" than to invite ridicule. I only knew that a greater force was opening up a whole Universe for me. And it did just that! I began to manifest all the things and people I needed just by holding on to a single thought. But I did not have complete control over this. It played havoc with my life! The Universe did not discriminate between what was "good" or "bad" unless I asked it to do that. I had understood the Principles of Hypnosis and Subconscious Reprogramming, having been a teacher of the subject and a Master Hypnotist for many years. But now helter skelter and willy nilly, manifestations were experienced on a daily basis. I learned to "control" and "steady" my thoughts and my emotions and began to teach others what I had learned. Then spontaneously again I started to remember the Realm and the teachings and truths I was exposed to. I was 'asked' to produce a movie and I was given a name "THE META SECRET". Many people and elements and forces who shall remain nameless for now tried to stop me from making this Movie and this Book possible.

I was brought to the edge of bankruptcy, went through a painful divorce, separated from the two munchkins who meant the whole world to me, endured the betrayal of friends, battled forces that meant me harm and became more emotionally-scarred than most ordinary people have a right to be.

Yet through it all, "something" stayed by my side and revealed its power to me slowly. I suddenly realized that I was NOT alone. But that is another story and another Book altogether. Regardless of what other people felt, I knew that I had to help everyone regardless of whether they positioned themselves as my "enemy" or friend. Feelings of love and compassion just flowed from me in gushes at inconvenient times, like in the middle of a heated business negotiation or contract violation. I would begin to feel the person we were in battle positions with. I began to see and feel their fears, pain, needs and their futures! I wrote and designed a poster to describe this overwhelming emotion. It goes like this: "WE ARE ALL ONE: If we could read the secret thoughts of our enemies, we would find in each person's life, a sorrow and a suffering deep enough to completely disarm all hostility."

That was when THE META SECRET began to reveal itself to me. All things came clearly into view. I understood who I was, where I was and what I had to do. The normal ways of thinking began to slip from me. A new perspective filled with possibilities and Laughter.

Part One

Meta is a nice word.
It's a word most people don't understand.

It's just what you can't see with your eyes.
You have to 'see' with your inner eye of understanding.

Meta' means beyond the physical.

Do you know that 99 % of our population has been programmed to let the outside world control the inside? If you want to get what you want, you have to let the inside world control the outside.

That's what the Meta Secret's all about.

Bob Proctor

CHAPTER 1
The Day the World Changed

Chapter 1

The Day the World Changed

"Time of death, 4.15 am!"

I can pinpoint that single moment in my life when the earth stood still, as if holding its breath to see how I would greet my destiny. I'm sure if a stopwatch had timed it, only a split second would have passed. Yet, in that instant, a new world opened up to me, hinting at the secrets of a knowing beyond knowing. Nothing would ever be the same. I somehow knew I was on no ordinary journey.

My name is Mel Gill, but most people just call me Mel. As a psychotherapist and motivational speaker I travel all over the world, talking to people about their subconscious minds and how thoughts not only determine levels of happiness but, inevitably, their destinies. It's a pretty cool job but, as I started to tell you, I know this because of my own journey—a journey I happened upon, quite literally, by accident.

The year was 1976 and I was 18 years old. Earlier in the day I'd been given a small, flat stone inscribed with a symbol that looked like an 'M'. It was a rune, a character from the Viking alphabet. But, unlike contemporary writing systems, ancient people ascribed great power to their letters. The name rune means 'secret'. To the ancients, the runes, originally consisting of 24 characters, often inscribed on small stones, were an oracle. They would put the runes in a bag or small container, mix them up and then draw a stone without looking, as a way of prophesying their future. By saying the name of a rune aloud, they invoked its vibration and the stone would 'aid' the seeker in their quest. Perhaps, that's why I carried the stone; I was searching for my path and what was to come next.

I was told that the rune I'd drawn and now carried was 'Ehwaz'. Some said the 'M' shape was symbolic of two horses' heads facing each other nose to nose, while others claimed it represented a rider on a horse. It stood for purposeful motion, forward progress and sometimes a journey, but not just of the physical realm. Ehwaz was a journey of the spirit. Just as a rider and horse must have a strong partnership, it is important for a body and soul to have a strong partnership. It symbolised that, in life, it is not enough to take care of the physical, if the mind and emotions are neglected.

As a first generation Indian American, the runic wisdom reminded me of a Hindu myth I'd heard long ago about the god Shiva and his second wife Parvati. After Shiva's first wife was murdered, he'd lost interest in the world.

Shiva had a very important role of 'Destroyer' and 'Protector' and was formerly known for having a terrible temper but, after losing the love of his life, he fell apart. Like many emotionally-injured humans, he decided the best course of action to keep himself from further pain, would be to avoid the physical world and his problems altogether. So, he withdrew to a mountaintop and began to meditate. After all, hanging out in the ethereal planes, learning from the Great Masters, was a much better gig and all around emotionally safer for him, or so he thought!

The only problem was, it also meant Shiva was neglecting his role as 'protector', among other things, in the physical realm. Everything went out of whack without him to help balance the world. The sun refused to shine, the crops began to die and chaos was closing in quickly. So the gods came up with a plan to help Shiva get his groove back. They created a new goddess, Parvati, to be his wife and lure him back down to Earth.

It was really tough going at first, but she didn't give up on him. Eventually, through time and patience, she got him back down to Earth and they struck a little deal. From time to time he could still go up and meditate with the Masters as long as he always came back down to spend some time with her too!

So, while Shiva is seen as the mental and emotional aspect of being human, Parvati is the physical. To be totally consumed by either mental or physical wants and desires neglects the balance of the Universe and makes everything unstable. Therefore, the goal of humans should be to strike a balance between the two.

Similarly, the essence of the rune Ehwaz was urging me to go beyond the physical, to go on a soul's journey to gain hidden wisdom and knowledge. Little did I know that powerful forces were already at work summoning the conditions that would allow me to connect with the opportunities that would set me on my life's path.

Though I was far from convinced of the power of runes, I thought Ehwaz was a good omen. It represented a man on a journey of discovery and that was exactly who I was.

My party and I were trekking through mountains in the jungles of Malaysia. The shadows of night had long since closed in on our little group, but we'd decided to keep traveling for a while. Suddenly, and without warning, I lost my footing and found myself plummeting down a steep slope. My heart raced as I flailed helplessly, desperately trying to break my fall. Momentum beyond my control hurtled me forward and I found myself flung about like a limp rag doll. Then, with a single loud crack, I slammed hard onto the stone floor of a deep grotto. Then everything went black.

My head was spinning as I came to. I was dizzy, nauseous and felt every inch of my body screaming in pain. It quickly became clear that I had several compound fractures in my left arm. With no way to communicate with the outside world, and no vehicles to move us through the dense vegetation, all we could do was press on. Over the next ten days, constant excruciating pain nearly overcame me as we hiked out of the jungle searching to find some semblance of medical help. By the time we reached a hospital, massive infections had all but consumed me.

The surgeon told my family to prepare for the worst. He was certain I wouldn't make it. Nonetheless, he would try to save me by amputating my dangerously-infected arm.

Then, without warning, it happened! I went from being overcome with fever and drunk with medication to complete clarity. Suddenly, I was outside my body looking down at myself and watching the surgeon prepare to amputate my arm. I was fully aware, as dual perception set in. One part of me felt the blades of the saw slice through my arm; vibrating against my bones as it did so; while the other half peered into my own face as I lay incoherent on the operating table. It was the weirdest sensation I have ever experienced; to see the face I'd known all my life, so alien and yet so familiar. More unnerving, perhaps, was the 'detached-curiosity' I was observing this with!

Then my mind split again; fragmenting into many pieces, each with total comprehension of individual scenes playing out around me, yet all viewed simultaneously. As I saw myself on the table, I could see my parents and siblings distressed and waiting in the other room outside, as well as other scenes in different parts of the hospital. I could hear and understand all the conversations at once.

"Holy crap," I thought. "What in the world is going on?" But before I had a chance to comprehend, a voice from the operating room spoke:

"Time of death 4:15 a.m."

"Wait!" I tried to scream, as my awareness centered on a nurse writing my time of death on a chart covered in clear cellophane. But I couldn't make them hear me. I no longer formulated words the way I once had, yet I could see and feel everyone's thoughts. Nothing made sense. I still existed, still had awareness, yet no idea who 'I' was anymore.

Yet, there was no time for contemplating this either because, in the next second, a great sucking vortex pulled me backwards through the ceiling and into the early morning sky. Physical familiarity faded around me as the perceptions of space such as up and down or near and far withdrew and dwindled out of my existence.

I next found myself traveling through a white multi-hued tunnel. A being in shimmering blue-violet light with a countenance of total love and benevolence appeared before me. Pure happiness and well-being filled my every molecule as all the good things from my life came flooding back to me at once. Without using words I could completely understand this being and knew that he totally accepted who I was and all I had done. Totally! Yet at the same time, it was as if we were a part of each other. He embraced me and my emotions ran raw. I cried and cried, happiness and relief pouring over me. I had an immense sense of peace and completeness. I was 'home'!

Then before I could do or think about this any further, he filled me with such an inner knowing that gently said it was not my time and that I still had many things left to do back on Earth. Always being one to bargain I pleaded, like a child at their favorite park, to stay for just a little while longer. With a wise and playful smile that reminded me of a Buddha statue I'd once seen, he laughed and granted my request. He left me with another being of light who gave me the immediate knowing that I was much loved.

She encompassed me in total bliss as we glided down the most beautiful flower-lined path. Because language was not used it is difficult to find the words to describe much of the wisdom she shared but she let me know that, when I returned here, all of Heaven would celebrate. Over the course of what felt like several days, she guided me through many classroom-like amphitheaters and I was flooded with the most incredible lessons. It seemed like hours, days passed. Yet, in the place where my body was lying, only a few minutes had actually passed.

As my time of death was called, something registered with me even as I was 'pulled' out of the room. I saw a ball of light enter the surgeon, galvanizing him into action. He called his team to action saying, "Let's try one more thing."

He took a long, hollow needle and jabbed it into my ankle and began to infuse me with a fresh supply of blood.

Then he commenced compressions on my chest to restart my heart, which had stopped beating.

With a sudden 'whoosh' I was yanked backwards into a 'confined' space, in which I struggled to breathe. Though I'd technically been dead for more than a quarter of an hour, I was back just like that!

I'd been on a journey that transcended time and space, yet realized it was only a taste. While I remembered the main events of the 'other side', the specific details of what I had learned in the amphitheaters faded like a beautiful dream, gone much too soon! All that remained was an instinctive feeling. If I was ever to recover such peace and know such wisdom on Earth, I would have to start at the beginning, like a baby just learning to walk. But I knew that there were clues hidden just beneath the surface, waiting for me to find them.

Needless to say, surviving what I had gave me a very different perspective on life. While I had vaguely suspected there was something more to human existence and the Universe before my ordeal, I now knew beyond knowing. Not only had I seen it with my own eyes, I felt with every fiber of my being.

Slowly, as I became even more physically aware, I realised that my fist was tightly grasping something, which cut into my palm. I raised my remaining hand and realized, somehow, I still held the rune of Ehwaz! I lifted it closer to examine the small stone. As it turned on its left side, I realized it became the Greek symbol for Sigma or self-energy - the sum of all secrets. I smiled and closed my eyes. As crazy as all this may sound, I knew that was exactly what I'd encountered. While I should have been mourning the loss of my limb, I realized that I had just gained something much more, and of unmeasured value.

Over the years I came to learn that I am one of a growing number of people who have experienced something similar. I was not alone! Some have encountered this phenomenon through an accident or illness, like me, while others are born with the gift. Still others have reached a level of spiritual advancement that has allowed them to gain access to this special place. Still, many others haven't experienced it, but instinct tells them there is something more to be found and so they have joined the search.

No one knows exactly why this movement towards enlightenment has been growing. Maybe we have reached a time in history when, as a collective, we are ready to take a quantum leap forward in social awareness. This in itself is no great secret. From the Hindu yugas to the Biblical book of Revelations, many cultures throughout history have foretold of such a time. The ancient Mayans spoke of this in terms of world ages. They believed that the Earth goes through cycles lasting 5,125 years each and contemporary science has now confirmed that the planet does indeed travel through the

Milky Way in an elliptical pattern lasting the same amount of time. As it reaches the furthest point out on that loop, Earth's magnetic pull decreases which, in turn causes a sense of disconnectedness. Though most people remain unaware of the why's, they nonetheless are affected by it, just as they are affected by the rhythms of day and night, or the moon's pull on the tide. This may also help to explain the recent influx of war, economic collapse and global warming. In essence, no matter how far science takes us, we are still susceptible to the laws of nature and a greater force.

But whatever the reason, the fact remains that a large number of people are searching for control over their own lives, true happiness and a sense of peace. There is an intrinsic desire to feel a connection to something beyond ourselves - or at least to know that we are not alone in feeling the way we do. We want to understand why things happen and how the Universe works. This search has led many people to the internet, TV, radio and books, hoping to find greater meaning to their lives, and a way to live more powerful, productive lives. One such book which many readers will be familiar with is 'ced *The Secret*'.

Since it was published in 2006, it has helped millions of people find greater clarity within their own lives. For those who aren't familiar, this best-selling book is based on the core principle of the Law of Attraction. However, most don't realize the Law of Attraction is just one in a set of seven ancient laws. Author Rhonda Byrne credits her inspiration to a book called *The Science of Getting Rich*, which was written over a century ago by Wallace Wattles. His book came out just two years after the first printed version of The Kybalion, written anonymously by Hermetic teachers who called themselves The Three Initiates. *The Science of Getting Rich* was based on the concept of positive thought and states that, by replacing negative thought patterns with positive ones, we give ourselves the power to change our lives.

This concept caught on quickly due to such new inventions as Alexander Graham Bell's telephone and Henry Ford's Model T, which were proving that ordinary men could use the power of their minds to become millionaires. The public became hungry for a set of rules to help them understand how they, too, could become rich. Soon a flood of books spilled onto the market, outlining various mystic principles and the New Thought Movement. The concept that 'thought determines reality' was born. This was truly exciting stuff because it was the first time that people, as a society, understood that they had the power to shape their futures.

Combine that with our modern emphasis on consumerism and those ideas from the New Thought Movement are again extremely attractive concepts. Therefore, when the Law of Attraction resurfaced in *The Secret*, the idea that we can have anything simply just by using our minds has become very appealing.

But while the Law of Attraction is a valid one, which does work, it's like only being served an appetizer at a banquet. Yes, it's delicious, but it's not meant to be a meal by itself. We don't look at an appetizer and say, "That was great but it didn't fill me up." We understand that it was only the beginning of a feast and that there are still many courses left to savor before we are full.

As a Therapist, lecturer and student of history who has observed human nature and people all over the world, it's disappointing to see that so many people have misunderstood the Law of Attraction and try to fill up on 'appetizers'. The Law of Attraction is much more than a get-rich-quick philosophy to help us visualize a mailbox full of cash and have it appear, or use penetrating thoughts to have Brad Pitt, Sandra Bullock fall in love with us - though it might be nice!

Using the Law of Attraction in this way reminds me of a scene from the first 'Austin Powers' movie in which Dr. Evil tries to hold the world ransom for - ONE MILLION DOLLARS! Embarrassed, his second-in-command must explain to the monetarily-challenged super-villain, recently cryogenically unfrozen from the sixties, that their own corporation makes $9 billion a year! In a similar way, using the Law of Attraction to acquire a few trinkets such as a new car or those earrings you really wanted falls vastly short of its greater potential, such as finding long-term peace and happiness.

Skeptics have said to me, "Dr. Mel, the Law of Attraction is a bunch of bunk. I've tried it and it just doesn't work. So why do you continue to promote this stuff?"

I tell them that if the Law of Attraction is consumed as only an appetizer, they're probably right. But these and thousands of other well-meaning souls are missing the larger picture - that there are universal laws that really do bring about prosperity. It's just that there's a little more to it than wanting something and asking for it.

Lets do a quick test that will illustrate this point. Think of a favorite memory. It can be anything positive, anything involving the best time you can ever remember. Imagine the scene before you - as if it were happening right now. How does it make you feel? More importantly, why do you feel that way? Do warm emotions, such as love, tenderness, or humor play key roles? Chances are the majority of you did not pick something to do with acquiring vast amounts of money, property, or other forms of wealth. But if it did, that's all right too. There's nothing wrong with prosperity and we will discuss this in more detail later. However, my point is that true happiness is linked to something more than just getting 'stuff'.

Real prosperity is much greater than the process of acquiring physical things, although it may encompass these as part of it. It is also about inner wealth, feeling love and compassion for yourself and others, being at peace and feeling relaxed, enjoying life and being truly happy. In other words, like the rune of Ehwaz that I drew so long ago, it comes back to that balance between the mental and physical. Simple? Seemingly.

Motivational speaker Joe Vitale says knowing the Law of Attraction is "like having the Universe as your catalog." And he's right; but to be more accurate, it's like having a limited membership card for an online catalog. You're allowed to see all the really cool things and can 'window' shop as much as you like, but, until you become a full member, you can only purchase selected items.

In order to reach our full potential, we need to understand the greater secret of how the Universe works. This secret is the secret beyond all secrets. It is the Meta Secret, or 'thinking beyond the secret'. As I stated earlier, the Law of Attraction is just one law within a group of seven Hermetic Laws. These laws are interlaced and *must* work in concert with each other to bring order to the Universe. Only by understanding and applying *all* of the laws do we find true and lasting happiness.

Asking for what you want is only part of the process; the other laws must be taken into consideration and positively applied to achieve consistent results. Therefore, by only consuming the appetizer portion of the meal, we may be briefly satiated, but we deny ourselves the pleasure and fulfilment of the entire meal.

The great thing about Hermetic Laws is that they are constant. Despite the fact that the world is always changing, these laws will always stay the same. Because they are the laws of the Universe, they are interwoven into the fabric of all cultures and all religions, so they apply evenly and without bias to everyone and everything regardless of age, race, sex, creed, or monetary status.

A perfect example of how these greater forces are at work in everything can be seen through a simple definition James Ray gives in *The Secret*. "It can never be created or destroyed, it always was, always has been, everything that ever existed always exists, it's moving into form, through form and out of form." While scientists would say this information defines energy, theologians would argue it describes God. Either way, it is a law of the Universe!

The wonderful thing about these laws is that we don't have to meditate for days on end, join a convent or monastery, or learn to play a harp in the clouds before we can have access to them - we just have to understand how they work. It's a little like reading the manual for a new cell phone. And I know I just committed a major violation of the code of brotherhood by writing such blasphemy. In fact, if you listen intently, I think you'll hear every guy in the entire world collectively groaning. After all, real men don't read instructions, they just do it! But have you ever noticed that if the instruction booklet happens to fall open and a guy 'accidentally' glances at it, that they start to realize that the phone can do so much more than just dial numbers? Pretty soon it can be used for just about anything: music, the internet, GPS, opening the garage door, fixing a flat tire, freezing time - well maybe not all those things but you get the idea. When we understand the instructions, we no longer have to randomly punch buttons and hope we find what we need, we can directly dial our heart's desires. The Meta Secret is the same thing. It's a lot easier to achieve what we want if we understand how universal law works.

No one knows where the Hermetic Laws really came from, but popular opinion holds that it originated from a guy named Hermes Trismegistus (TRIES-MAH-GEEST-US). He was an ancient Egyptian philosopher and spiritual leader. Among other credits on his resume, he is said to be the founder of astrology and alchemy, as well as a contemporary and perhaps teacher of the Biblical patriarch Abraham.

In any case, he was so wise that people began to compare him with the Greek messenger god, Hermes, or the Egyptian god of mysticism, Thoth. For all intents and purposes, he was the rock star of his day.

In addition to setting ancient Egypt on its ear with radical new ideas, legend says that Hermes inscribed his wisdom onto a large green stone known as The Emerald Tablet or Tabula Smaragdina. It was a kind of recipe book containing seven formulae for reaching a higher degree of understanding and wisdom through altered states of consciousness. It's been said that these formulas applied simultaneously to mental, physical and spiritual reality to create a greater understanding. This helps explain why he was given the nickname 'Trismegistus' meaning three-times great. His followers believed if a new reality could be achieved by a large enough group of people, human evolution would be accelerated.

One of the most famous quotes from the Tablet is "As above, so below." Because the information contained within the texts was to help humanity heal and balance, it is believed it was inscribed onto a green stone, which is symbolic of the fourth chakra and healing the heart.

But not everyone was so enamored with the general public having access to such 'dangerous knowledge'. Remember, until recently, most of humanity was governed by monarchies. If people began to think too much for themselves, it would be very difficult to control the masses. Therefore, most officials didn't like the idea of a tablet floating around out there that might possibly usurp their power.

They couldn't risk people gaining access to such dangerous knowledge. From the priests of ancient Egypt to the monasteries of the Middle Ages, religious leaders quickly dispensed with anyone who breathed a word of the Emerald Tablet by accusing them of being heretics or witches - the penalty for which was hanging or beheading.

Feeling rather attached to their heads, Hermetists came up with a plan of their own. They vowed to study the laws of the Emerald Tablet in secret. Information was then either memorized or hidden within poems, paintings, or other works of art. Naturally, no one was privy to these highly-guarded secrets without first undergoing initiation and purification rites. Hermetists were so tight-lipped with their information that we now have a contemporary phrase 'hermetically sealed' to denote tightly secured items.

The Emerald Tablet was last seen around the time of Alexander the Great, when it was translated into Greek and openly displayed in Egypt. Because the conqueror was a fan, Hermetic philosophy enjoyed a brief period of 'being in the open' and was absorbed into the mystical teachings of both Judaism and Alexandrian Gnosticism (a branch of Christianity). However, the Tablet disappeared about a hundred years later when legend has it that its caretakers buried it to protect it from zealots who were ransacking and burning many important centers of learning.

However, the loss of the Tablet could not destroy the Hermetic Laws. The thing about Universal law is that it is everywhere; it exists anyway, whether it is written down or not. Keepers of the wisdom simply went underground. Along the way, several secret societies such as the Knights Templar and Freemasons sprang from the oral traditions of the Hermetic principles known as The Kybalion. The Kybalion simply refers to the verbal body of Hermetic phrases, principles and anecdotes handed down through the generations. One such phrase states, "Where fall the footsteps of the Master, the ears of those ready for his Teaching open wide," while another says, "The lips of Wisdom are closed, except to the ears of Understanding."

These secret societies understood that, while it would be ideal to share their information with everyone, fear plays a powerful role in what people are willing to learn and accept. If something is seen as threatening, human instinct is to lash out or recoil - not accept it openly. Because of this, Hermetists understood that wisdom could not be forced, but that, when people were ready to learn, the laws of the Universe would bring the Hermetic principles to them. Therefore, we can conclude that by reading this book, *you* are open. You are ready to learn and so the Meta Secret will be revealed to you. By doing so, you join the company of famous Hermetists such as Roger Bacon, Isaac Newton and Carl Jung.

So what is the Meta Secret and how exactly does it work? The Meta Secret is not a single method or system. It is a combination of Universal law, tools and methodologies. In the brief minute that I was on the 'other side', I learned about the vastness of a world far beyond human comprehension. While much of it was buried in the deep recesses of my subconscious when I returned to this side, some things remained within my memory and which I will never forget. With these clues, I began a journey that has spanned my lifetime to uncover these precious lessons once again and truly understand why life on Earth works the way it does.

The answers are hidden all around us, but they are only revealed to those who understand that the wisdom of the world will only be shared when you quiet yourself to listen to what the Earth has to say and when you let your ego fall away so that your true self can shine through.

As you'll see in the coming chapters; with deeper examination; The Meta Secret reveals the hidden truths of the Universe and all the power that goes with it.

This is the story of my search and how I came to know the Meta Secret...

CHAPTER 2
Anything Is Possible

CHAPTER 2
Anything Is Possible

Not long after my accident and when I had healed, I resumed my journey but this time I wasn't floundering for my life's purpose, I was on a mission! At my core level I was aware of all the wonderful knowledge I had learned on the other side. It was like having the answers to the why's and how's of the Universe on the tip of my tongue, yet not being able to fully materialize them. It was maddening to know I knew and yet not be able to access the information. That energy fueled my passion to find and crystallize those answers into a body of information that I could fully use on this side and share with others to help make life easier. That is why I began to call this information the Meta Secret, because it truly was a secret beyond all secrets, once revealed, then hidden again, only to be truly understood when it was uncovered through experience. I found that many, even after reading and learning of it, could not understand it's workings and so, for them, it still remained a secret!

That was the lesson of the other side - things which come to us automatically there must be learned and experienced to be understood here. It's one thing to know something in your head and quite another to fully implement it with your heart. And so I searched the great libraries of the world, visited exotic locations and interviewed all the leading experts in an effort to find the Meta Secret.

I'm not sure what it was exactly, but something kept telling me to trust my instincts; let my intuition be my guide and the information I was seeking would find me. Little did I know at that point that this was the Law of Attraction in Action - the simple law of the Universe which says that like always attracts like. Therefore, positive will attract positive, negative will attract negative.

The first key in my search came when I was introduced to the Hermetic Laws many years ago. I knew they were something important but their true significance would take a while to click. As I said, it's one thing to intellectually know something, but often experience is really the best teacher.

As I begin to share this information with you, I offer full disclosure: *The Meta Secret* will never change your life if all you plan to do is read it. To truly change your life, you must internalize this information, make it your own, implement it. Understand that this will not be an overnight sensation for most people; it is a gradual process of small changes over time. Master violinists do not become brilliant overnight; baseball players practice to excel at the game; doctors must attend years of school and training before they perform surgery - and so it will be with you. Know that there are no quick fixes. But, if you are worth investing in - and I think you are - then the process will be worth it. It will be an exciting journey and I am honored to be a part of it.

Have you ever had a dream which seemed so real you weren't sure where it ended and reality began? And, even though you'd never met the characters in it before, they felt very familiar? Such a dream is a little like the Law of Mentalism, the first of the seven Hermetic Laws. It says, "The All is Mind: The Universe is Mental." Though it might sound loopy at first, remember ancient Hermetists wanted to appear a little nuts, just in case they were found out! Better to be thought harmless, crazy men than hung as heretics!

Our dreams are a good analogy for this first law because, when we dream we become like the 'All'. We create whole worlds', complete with landscapes, buildings, people and anything else we can imagine. While we are dreaming, those things feel very real and separate from ourselves yet, in reality, they are our creations. And so, technically, all those things are simply versions of us. Therefore, while dreaming is an analogy, it is also part of a larger concept in which our waking thoughts help to create our realities.

We see evidence of this every day. Anyone who holds a particular thought in their head and then acts upon it *is* creating their own reality. A wonderful example of this comes from Bill Gates. Back in the 1970s at Harvard, he and Paul Allen worked on an early version of computer programming. Through this project he came to believe that every home and business should have a computer. So he set about finding a way to do just that. During his junior year of college, he finally gathered enough information and assets to make his dream come true. And so he left school to start Microsoft. I don't have to tell you, his thought became reality; nearly everyone in developed countries has used one or more of his products.

The Law of Mentalism was at work for Bill Gates. But it only worked because, whether he was aware of it or not, he employed the other laws of the Universe to work in concert with it. He didn't just say, "I hope people will someday find a way to bring computers into their homes and businesses," and then forgot about it. He took additional steps to make his thought a reality.

Let's transfer this concept to our own lives. How many of you have achieved great things in your lives because you didn't believe in yourselves or didn't think your dreams were possible? Probably not too many. Everything we do; or don't do; is because of the Law of Mentalism. If you believe you can ride a bicycle, you will. If you believe you can pass a test, you will. If you believe you can bake a cake, you will. That's because when we believe something to be true or untrue, we act in certain ways that bring those thoughts to fruition.

When we tell our kids, "You can be anything you want," it really is true. When we say, "Anything is possible," that really is true too. That's because the mind is always creating and there is nothing that we can't think of. So if we can think of it, it is possible - maybe not today or tomorrow, but somewhere, somehow, someone will take that idea and make it real. Back in the 1960s, characters on the TV show *Star Trek* used tricorders to communicate with each other, look up important information and log data. At the time, such tools seemed like wonderful fictional magic, but today we call them Blackberries or multimedia devices!

Hermes used deductive reasoning when he wrote the Law of Mentalism: he reasoned that the only thing that always stays the same is change. The Universe or the All is always changing because, in order to exist, it must create. So, because we are all part of the Universe, we change through creating. The tool we use to create change is our minds; therefore, our thoughts create our realities.

If it's not quite clear yet, that's alright. The writers of The Kybalion thought this law was so important that they spent the first four chapters on it, while giving only one additional chapter to the other laws. Without understanding this law, it's difficult to understand the others. But, while it may be a little fuzzy, you probably know a lot more about it than you realize. That's because the Law of Mentalism is found throughout history and pop culture.

Remember the '80s song *We Are the World*, in which several American performers banded together in a super-group to help raise money for Africa? Its chorus says: *We Are the World, We are the children, We are the ones who make a brighter day...* For younger people, the theme song from the Disney classic *The Lion King* says something similar: *It's the Circle of Life and it moves us all, Through despair and hope, Through faith and love...* Both these songs are saying that we are all part of the same energy, an energy we create through our actions.

So the first part of the Law of Mentalism is saying we are all connected to each other. That's a theme we can all identify with. President Barack Obama even used the slogan 'We are One' for his inauguration. That sense of unity hung thick in the air for Americans after the 9/11 attacks on the World Trade Center and the Pentagon. Others have felt overwhelming unity following the Sichuan Province earthquake, the Indonesian Tsunami, or the Chernobyl Disaster, just to name a few. During these times, we let our guards down and we see each other for who we really are. We can look into the face of a man or woman no matter their age and see a vulnerable child. We will hug a complete stranger, or pat them on the back, just to connect with one another. During these times, we realize that we really are not so different from each other. At the basic core level, we are the same. We all breathe the same air, we all must have shelter, eat, sleep and, in the end, none of us gets out of this earthly experience alive!

Ideally, we would always be able to see this about each other. This is actually the way we come into the world. As babies, our first awareness is not of ourselves but of others around us. Small children do not see themselves as separate from their mothers. We first begin to notice toddlers developing their own sense of awareness around the age of two. Jokingly, we refer to this stage as 'the terrible twos' because no one will ever be able to control that child again! Just imagine how pleasant things might be if we could extend that sense of oneness in our children until they were 18. Of course, then we'd just have the terrible 20s, which might not be so practical. At least when two-year-olds throw temper tantrums, we can pick them up and remove them from the situation. Most of us just aren't made to lug 150-pound sons out of the toy store if they don't get what they want.

Over time, we begin to form an awareness of ourselves, based on our experiences with the world. Experiences help us to shape our likes and dislikes, as well as our hopes, dreams and memories; with this information we decide where to live, who we live with, what to do for a living and so on and so forth. Pretty soon we begin to define ourselves by those experiences. I am a doctor, a mother, a surfer and so on. While these things form the basis of our personalities or egos, most people mistake these experiences for their identities. The difference is, while these things describe you, they are not you. The meal is not the menu!

As we move through life, we identify so strongly with all these things which get caught up in our egos, that we lose sight of our true essence - the part of ourselves that feels connection to everyone and everything else. Author and educator, John Bradshaw once explained this by saying, "Ego is to the True Self what a flashlight is to the spotlight."

Disasters have a way of peeling back our egos to reveal who we really are once more. At our base level, our true selves are all still connected and so when something horrible happens that's who we become. In the *Wizard of Oz*, Dorothy expresses this feeling many times throughout the movie when she says, "I just want to go home." Many of us say something similar when we are faced with uncertainty or danger. We just want to go home. Why? Because home is safety. Instinctively, we know that our true selves are the safest places to be, at that level we are pure love, peace and joy. Nothing bad can happen there because we are the creators of our universe and so, instinctively, we know that's where we need to go to be safe when something terrible happens. Instinctively, we know that all the other junk our egos have us carry around - that part of us that says we should never be friends with someone different or give them the time of day, that says my job is so much more advanced than yours, that my religion is so much more enlightened than yours, that I'm so much more sophisticated than you - doesn't really matter in the end. It's not important because according to the laws of the Universe we are all the same because we are all susceptible to the same forces. So when an earthquake hits, or terrorists strike, or any number of other disasters happen, our awareness becomes the same and so we become indistinguishable from one and other. Our identities and awareness are the same. At a basic level, we are all a part of each other (the All) because we share an indistinguishable awareness (the Mind) that forms the foundation for everything in existence (the Universe).

"Stress is caused, in my opinion, when we take our power and give it to the problem. We want to maintain the power. I AM IN CONTROL OF ME. The power is going to stay with me! I am not going to let the condition, the circumstance, or the challenge that I may be facing control me! You can make a decision right now that you are going to maintain your power. You're going to let everything outside stay outside. Just remember that when you're in a totally relaxed state the solution to your problem comes!

Quit getting involved in these sophisticated stress management deals. Release the stress! Let it go. You are in charge of your body. Just say "Peace." Be still. Visualize a beautiful lavender energy flowing right into the crown of your head and circulating right through your body and then start to imagine every molecule of your body vibrating in perfect harmony with God's Laws. You're totally relaxed. You're in charge of yourself. There is no stress where there is relaxation.

Take control of your life and its starts in your mind. This is the Meta Secret."

The All goes by many names. Yes, we are a part of the All, but it is also much more. It is Life and Mind, some call it Spirit, others say it is God, The Absolute Truth, The Creator, The Father, Mother Nature, or even Energy. Summum philosophy, which draws on Hermetic wisdom, calls the All 'a union between nothing and all possibility, the ultimate opposites, with no beginning and no end that simply created each other to form the infinite living mind.'

Whatever you may call it, the concept of 'separate yet one' is a little tricky to comprehend. It's kind of like looking at one of those computer-generated pictures from the '90s that at first just looks like several dots, but later when you learn to relax and see with greater vision, you realize it's a 3-D image.

One of the easiest examples of how this Law of Mentalism is always at work around us comes from world religions. Judaism uses the concept with the doctrine 'God Was, Is and will always Be.' Christianity describes God as three-in- one; Father, Son and Holy Ghost. Likewise, many pagans have three aspects of the creator in maiden, mother and crone. Further back, ancient Egyptians also used several trinities such as Osiris, Isis and Horus. Hinduism does something similar describing Brahma as one god, with thousands of avatars, such as Krishna, Kali and Vishnu, to describe different aspects.

Interestingly, this concept of separate and yet one is also present in science. While Einstein was never able to prove his universal theory, quantum entanglement, the Heisenberg Uncertainty Principle and several other sub-atomic theories which follow similar statements, have proven to be real.

Being separate and yet one is a difficult concept to grasp. The authors of The Kybalion explained it by saying a foot is part of the body, but it's not the whole body. It can even be said that, in a sense, striving to understand the Law of Mentalism is one of the oldest quests on Earth because it is a search to understand ourselves and how we all fit together - in other words, our oneness. It can be seen in stories told since the beginning of recorded time. The *Iliad*, *King Arthur's Tales* and *Alice in Wonderland* are all examples. Hollywood even has a categorical name for these stories. They're known as quests.

"According to the tradition that I come from, happiness is a function of accepting what's so. It says in the Torah that the one who is happy is content with his lot. But that is not in any way, shape, or form to be confused with passive acceptance of the status quo or resignation.

There is a call to action. It's kind of a paradox. You should absolutely work toward improving your life, improving the world, improving your finances, improving your relationships, every sort of conceivable improvement at a micro or macro level should indeed be your agenda.

But, if you are not happy with things the way they are now, then your happiness is perpetually on hold pending a condition that doesn't exist yet. If you do that, you will never be happy."

In *Hitchhiker's Guide to the Galaxy,* the characters are sent on what seems like an impossible quest for a crazy president, who wants them to find the answer to the meaning of life, the Universe and everything in it. Throughout the story, the characters meet with several hardships and struggles before finally finding a super-computer which is supposed to give them the answer to the meaning of life. The computer emphatically tells them the answer is 42! This of course doesn't sit well with the characters because it doesn't make sense. Things go seemingly from bad to worse when they learn their world has been created by a couple of mice as an amusement. But in the end, their adventure teaches them that none of this matters because they have found happiness.

A friend of mine took her two young sons to see this comedy. As they walked back to the car, her nine-year old said, "I think that means the meaning of life is what you make it." His wiser thirteen-year old brother shook his head in disagreement, "If that's really true, why would anyone make it something they don't want?"

Why indeed? They were both right. The Law of Mentalism tells us that because the universe is in our minds, we can create whatever we want. The caveat is that the Law of Attraction will draw to us whatever we mentally project. So if we want a lasting romantic relationship, but believe that all women are gold-diggers or all men are chauvinists, we are concentrating our energy on the qualities we *don't* want. The Law of Attraction doesn't take likes or dislikes into account. It simply brings to us whatever we project. Negative thoughts will attract more negative experiences, positive thoughts will attract positive experiences. Therefore, if we concentrate on projecting the qualities in ourselves that we want to find in a mate, that person will come to us. In this scenario, it becomes easy to see how the laws of the Universe start to work together. Our mind creates whatever we want, which in turn helps us to act in certain ways, which helps bring that which we want to us.

Because we are constantly creating and therefore constantly changing, we are also constantly learning. Sometimes these changes happen in quantum leaps and sometimes they happen very slowly. So, from time to time, we stop to evaluate this process of change and decide if we are pleased with where our mental creations are taking us. As we discussed earlier, we try it out first as small children differentiating ourselves from our mothers, then as teenagers trying to figure out just where we fit into the world and often again in midlife. We may not know exactly what we're doing when we go through these periods of assessment, but universal law instinctively governs us all to take stock. While it may be easy to blame others or a set of circumstances for all our misfortunes and misadventures, once we realize that the Law of Mentalism puts us in total control of our futures and destinies, we truly become free to create the lives we have always wanted.

This leads us to the question that if we are creating everything and so is everyone else, then some things must not be real. "Either I am right, or they are right." This is part of the universal Law of Paradox, which says that everything in the Universe is an illusion and, at the same time, it is real. It uses another of the seven laws called the Law of Polarity, which says that opposites are really different degrees of the same thing. We'll examine this in a coming chapter. For now the important thing is that there's a big difference between absolute truth and personal truth.

The All knows absolute truth, but as individuals we all have personal truths as we experience them. That's why people who witness an accident can all give different accounts of what happened and all be correct. We believe our senses tell us what is real and what isn't. We have to trust that, otherwise, as a physical being on the planet Earth, it would be very difficult to get through the day. We need those perceptions to learn our lessons and continue to create our world. Could you imagine what would happen if we all believed tornadoes were an illusion and walked headlong into them? Or decided that we didn't need to breathe air and went scuba diving without an oxygen tank? We wouldn't make it very far, would we? We gain control over our lives by accepting that there is a physical world and that we are working with it. Then we apply the universal laws and use them with each other to achieve our individual goals.

"*One of the most important things you need to do in life is discover your purpose. I believe that everybody is born with an individual and unique purpose and when you are living your life purpose, when you are expressing and fulfilling it, you're happy.*

So many people have talked about joy being your guidance system - that when you're off purpose, it's telling you, "You are not happy, not joyful." And so this joy, this inner experience of happiness and joy is a way of saying, "Ooh I'm on course, I'm doing the things I'm supposed to do."

Think about it like this, a rose has to be a rose; a chrysanthemum has to be a chrysanthemum; a geranium has to be geranium they can't be a dandelion or something else. And yet, we as people have been given choice. The choice to pursue any number of things and do whatever we want to do, but unfortunately most of us have been talked out of our purpose."

The Three Initiates explained this process in the following way - *If humans act and live as if the Universe is only a dream, then they're like sleep-walkers stumbling through life and making no progress. They're forced awake when the natural laws, which they try to ignore, bruise them. Keep your mind ever on the star, but let your eyes watch over your footsteps, to avoid falling, should your focus be too far upward. The fact is that you are on Earth now and you must deal with its nature and laws. You can, however, enjoy your life if you work with the mental laws, which are higher than material laws.*

Later they went on to explain that we must change the way we view the world and use universal law, not denial, to create our reality. The only way we can create our own reality is through the use of our ego. In order to know what is true, we must know what isn't true. In other words, we learn reality by understanding those things which aren't real. By knowing what is false, the truth eventually reveals itself.

The human spirit also works with this polarity. You come into the world as a being connected to everyone and everything else as your true self, then you develop an ego through perceptions. In order to get back to your true self and that feeling of connectedness and oneness, you must go through a period of letting the ego go. It's a period of externalizing things again. Let's use the old boy scout example of helping an elderly person cross the street. If you do it for the recognition and because you hope to earn a merit badge, or because it makes you feel good, you are doing it for your ego. If you do it because the person really could use a hand and it will make their day a little easier, then you are doing it for your true self.

As the Indian mystic, Osho, once said of finding your true self, "Once you come near it, everything changes, everything settles again. But now this settling is not done by the society. Now everything becomes a cosmos, not a chaos; a new order arises. It is the very order of existence itself."

Now you may be asking, "What is the benefit of doing these altruistic things?" Life's difficult enough. I can barely keep up with myself, let alone helping everyone else. Yet this is also part of universal law and an exercise in polarity. When you let yourself go and just do, you get into the flow of life and relax into your true self. When you find your true self, that part of you that is connected to the Universe, you will be at peace. Happiness, love, joy, all the good things in life will come easily to you.

The interesting thing is that this again brings the Law of Paradox into play. We are already our true selves and so we must first accept that we are absolutely perfect just as we are. The key is that we must learn where to place our awareness in our mind, body, the world, or in all three, which gives us the greatest understanding of how to use the laws. And that will take some practice!

When Hermes wrote "As above, so below" on The Emerald Tablet, it was his way of letting people know that if they understood the seven laws on one plane of existence, they could understand them on all planes. We will discuss this more in the next chapter, however, this idea helps to explain the Law of Mentalism. So when we create reality with our thoughts, we are using mentalism. If we as humans are doing it, it stands to reason that the All is also doing it, which brings us full circle to the beginning of this chapter. Perhaps what you have read is only a life-like dream! After all, the Universe and everything in it is a mental creation. The All is Mind; The Universe is Mental.

"If we're talking about the metaphysical, we're talking about beyond the physical.

So, what we've got to do is go inside. We've been programmed to lure from the outside in. We're letting what's going on outside of us control what's going on inside.

If we're going to get into the meta side of our own personality, we've got to get away from this physical instrument we've got and move into the higher side of our own personality and start to understand that we live *simultaneously on three planes of understanding*. And we work from a higher to a lower potential. If you're working with electricity, any electrician, any engineer will tell you that you have to work from higher to lower potential. If you go contrary to that, you're not going to get any useful purpose or use out of the electricity.

When you're working with the mind you don't start with the physical and work up. You start with thought and work down. Thoughts are of a spiritual nature. Spirits are omni-present. Where are thoughts? Thoughts are omni-present.

One hundred percent may even be present in all places at the same time. I can be underwater and think. I can be in an airplane and think.

I got the pleasure of working with a couple of the astronauts that have been on the other side of the moon and they could think. Not only could they think on the other side of the moon, but they can transfer their thoughts to somebody here on Earth! It's just a form of telepathic communication."

CHAPTER 3

What Goes Around, Comes Around

CHAPTER 3
What Goes Around, Comes Around

The blade of the knife glinted in the candlelight, as an elderly man in robes approached me. "Give me your hand."

With uncertainty, I extended it towards him.

In one clean, swift gesture, he pierced my index finger. I tried to pull back, but his grip was firm as he squeezed a single drop of crimson to the surface and smiled.

"Do you know why this is so precious?" he asked.
"It's my blood," I swallowed, not sure if he meant to take more.
"Yes, but not just your blood. This," he chuckled, as he lightly lifted the drop onto his knife, "is the secret to the Universe. Not only is everything about you - your entire code contained in each and every drop - but it also contains the code for the entire Universe."
I shook my head, "I don't understand."
"You will," he said as he faded to transparency.
"Wait," I called, but the foggy mist of waking was swirling around me.

I lay in bed for a few long moments trying to hold on to the dream, however the more I thought about it, the less I remembered. Hurriedly, I scrambled to find a notebook and quickly scribbled, 'My blood, code to the Universe.' I stared at the phrase for a while. It did make sense; every drop of blood contains its owner's genetic code or DNA. Following the Law of Mentalism, if we are all part of each other and the Universe, then it followed that we also contain all the information of the Universe within us.

I remembered once hearing the late astronomer, Carl Sagan, say something about us all being made of 'star stuff'. He explained that, like stars, we are composed of carbon, nitrogen and oxygen, as well as many other things. But even more importantly than just sharing similar elements, when a star reaches the end of its life, it very often explodes. As that happens it sprinkles the Universe with tiny particles of itself, which astronomers call 'dust' or stardust. Because the Universe is the original recycler, it reuses whatever it can when creating new planets and solar systems. So everything on Earth, oceans, mountains, trees and even you and I, is created from that stardust!

The more I thought about it, the more I realized that there was something more to it than just the Law of Mentalism at work. While it made for many interesting discussions, it didn't provide a great deal of help for the everyday world, beyond understanding the other laws of the Universe.

This dream extended to the next law, the Law of Correspondence. Examining my blood to understand the Universe was just another way of explaining the second law. But instead of saying 'as above, so below,' I needed to tweak the phrase to say 'as within, so without.'

When Hermes carved those famous words into the Emerald Tablet, he was trying to explain that in order to understand the Universe, we need to know ourselves first. If we go inside ourselves, we can find the answers to everything, because everything we need is already inside us.

Just like the Law of Mentalism, the Law of Correspondence works on all three planes: mental, physical and spiritual. The only difference between these planes is that they vibrate at different speeds. The physical plane vibrates slower than the mental plane. You have witnessed this countless times in your own life. Many of us have had the experience of feeling like an accident was happening in slow motion. In the time it took for the misadventure to happen, a million thoughts spun through your head. Or, how many times have you been able to think the exact same thing as a friend in the split-second before they said it? Likewise, the mental plane vibrates slower than the spiritual plane. The energy of forgiveness, too, has a way of doing this, sometimes literally transforming the whole demeanor of the forgiven person.

"A lot of people spend valuable time in their lives focusing on their pasts. I have. I could probably spoil your week if I reviewed the first 26 years of my life. It was a mess!

When I was 26, I had a guy look at me and tell me that I was the most miserable person he had ever met! He was right. I was plain miserable. He said "you're always sick!" I didn't have a terminal illness or anything but I always had a backache, headache, or something and I was always broke. He said "why don't you change it?" Well, as long as I kept focusing on what led me to this point, I was going to create more of the same. He said "Let it go! Forgive it!"

The Law of Correspondence works across all planes in the same way, so the same laws of the Universe apply, no matter which plane we're dealing with. The Three Initiates explained it like this:

These divisions are artificial and arbitrary, because the three planes are ascending degrees of the scale of life, from the lowest point of matter to the highest point of Spirit. The different planes shade into each other, without hard distinctions between the higher phenomena of the physical and the lower phenomena of the mental, for example. In short, the Three Great Planes are groupings of the degrees of life manifestation.

The planes are neither places nor dimensions of space. Yet, they are more than states or conditions. The planes don't have the ordinary dimensions of length, depth and breadth, but they do have a "fourth dimension" of vibration.

This idea of three planes of existence is a strong theme in both Christianity as well as Judaism. We know them as the Earth, Heaven and Hell. Just like the Initiates mention a fourth dimension, the Catholic Church has a fourth dimension known as purgatory. But the similarities don't end there. Hermetists often make things a bit more complicated by introducing seven minor planes and seven sub-planes within each of the three major planes. Don't worry, we won't get into that, few people do these days. The levels within levels mostly serve as tools of learning for theoretical discussions and study. However it is interesting to note that Islam recognizes seven heavens and universes, while Buddhism also cites several planes of existence within the reincarnation process.

The Law of Correspondence is even at work on itself as we find correspondence between religion and science. Nearly a hundred years ago, a young German-Jew with a great passion for physics set out to prove that four-dimensional space-time exists and became hailed as one of the greatest scientists of all time. To this day, Albert Einstein's Theory of Relativity is known throughout the world. But he didn't stop there. Later as a professor at Princeton, he and an associate Nathan Rosen continued to explore the possibilities of the universe and came up with the Einstein-Rosen Theory which explains how different dimensions are seamlessly connected to each other.

Have you ever stood at the foot of a high-rise building and suddenly realized how small you were in comparison, or gazed up at the sky and felt dwarfed in its vastness? When we realize that these situations are still a very, very small corner of the Universe, it makes the task of understanding the All and everything in it seem insurmountable. But the really cool thing about the Law of Correspondence is that it has a built-in safety 'device' to help everyone understand it. That's because no matter if the thing we are trying to understand is larger than we could ever fully grasp or smaller than we can see with the naked eye, no matter which plane it exists on, everything is made up of the same stuff, the All. Because of this, everything is a reflection or replica of everything else.

A Yale math professor was able to prove this concept in the 1970s when he created a new way of doing geometry with something called fractals. Benoit Mandlebrot figured out that while some patterns like the sections of a pinecone, petals on a dandelion, or the division of butterfly wings could be explained to a point with regular geometry, most of nature uses irregular patterns called fractals. The key to finding the geometric formula for these seemingly irregular patterns, such as the branches of a tree or the spots on a leopard, was to realize that what we perceive as nonsense patterns were actually patterns within patterns within patterns! Sometimes these patterns aren't detected until the microscopic level, but they do exist. Down to the smallest of molecules the patterns are self-similar - or corresponding, which means that nature is not as random as we once believed.

We can see some of these patterns when looking at our own bodies. The sections of our fingers are cylindrical shaped, which fit into a joint, forming our fingers. That pattern continues with our hands which fit into our wrists, which fit into our elbows and so on. All of which just goes to show, whether we're aware of it or not, the laws of the Universe are constantly influencing us.

Because it is sometimes easier to come to terms with something when we take ourselves and our emotions out of the equation, humans have long used the Law of Correspondence as a learning tool in the form of stories. We know them as allegories, fables and parables. People throughout the world are familiar with Aesop's fables of *The Boy Who Cried Wolf* and *The Tortoise and the Hare*, as well as the Bible's parables of *The Mustard Seed* and *The Prodigal Son*. More recently, J.J.R. Tolkien's *Lord of the Rings* and C. S. Lewis' *The Lion, the Witch and the Wardrobe* have done a wonderful job of looking at what happens when we treat others poorly because they are different from us. Likewise, they also carry strong messages of good triumphing over evil when we take control of our lives and our destinies through positive thought and action.

"You know, it's been said that if you build it they will come. I think if you build it and you build something with true excellence and you distinguish it in the marketplace and you come up with a selling proposition and you are aggressive in your marketing to the world, it's possible that people will come. But it's not inevitable that they will come. Sitting around passively visualizing things is not likely to get the world beating a path to your door. You must take steps to help create your reality."

So what does the Law of Correspondence have to do with the everyday world in which we must take care of our families, earn a living and be all-round super-human? Quite a lot. That's because we are like gigantic mirrors reflecting everything that goes on inside us out into the world. Voilà, another pattern!

If you think about a person who's in love, you can see this pattern very quickly. They don't even have to be in love with a romantic partner - it can be a pet, a new baby, even themselves. I didn't say we all have to see it just to think about someone like this! When someone has true passion about something or someone, how do they act? They smile and they're happy. When someone is sincerely happy, that feeling is infectious. It's difficult to be a real grouch around someone who's happy. We may have a million other emotions tumbling around inside us, but it's not about us right now, we'll deal with that in a minute. Right now we want to focus on the happy people. Happy people feel good about themselves and so that reflects out into the world. That positive energy attracts both the people and situations to them which they desire. They get a raise at work, win a dream vacation for two, hear from a long-lost friend and so on. Even when things don't go as they planned, they're caught in traffic or dinner gets a little over-cooked, they don't sweat the small stuff. It just isn't that important to them because they realize that life is good and things will all work out.

But then there's the saying 'When it rains, it pours!' Because the laws of the Universe are neutral, they work in either direction. So if you have a rough night's sleep and then trip over the cat as you get out of bed and then kick him because he shouldn't have been there anyway, only to realize that you're late for work because the alarm didn't go off, so you don't shower which makes you look the way you feel - which makes you feel even worse because you know it's going to be a rotten day and sure enough by the time you get to work, you've missed an important meeting and the boss is fuming, so you take it out on your girlfriend when she calls and she cancels your date because you're acting like a jerk, only to have that annoying mother call to guilt you about being a bad son, because you haven't come over to help her with some project she's been bugging you about for months and then you arrive home as the firemen are clearing the smoke from your now soot-filled apartment, because in your hurry to leave you left the iron on and now the cat is gone and you melt down because you realize the last thing you did was kick her and she was the only one who ever really loved you! What a lot of drama!

Sometimes having laws apply equally is just a little fairer than we would like. So without playing favorites, the only way to move from a negative situation to a positive is for something to happen that shifts the paradigm. That shift comes when we change the way we view the world and our actions.

The reason so many addictions continue, whether it is shopping, drinking, or gambling, is because the person is trying to fix themselves from the outside, instead of going within. It never is about buying stuff or liking the taste of alcohol; rather, at a deeper level, there is always something more going on with that person. The person may not even be aware that their addictive bahavior is a way to suppress something deeper. However, no amount of changing the outside will ever be enough if we don't work on the inside. In a nutshell, that's what most self-help programs try to teach.

When Mahatma Gandhi said, "You must be the change you wish to see in the world," he was citing the Law of Correspondence. He knew that if we want to change the world, we must begin with ourselves by changing the way we think.

This reminds me of a Buddhist fable. Once there was a very wealthy man. When it came to money, he was like the Donald Trump of his day. And yet he was very miserly. He was such a penny-pincher that he could barely justify spending money on food, which of course would mean losing a small part of his fortune. Instead, he nearly starved himself as well as his wife, children and the servants.

One day while out on a walk, he met a boy selling sweet dumplings. They smelled so heavenly that he almost bought one, but at the last second he restrained himself. By the time he got home he wanted a sweet dumpling so badly that he made himself sick and went straight to bed. Soon his wife came to see what was wrong and he told her about the sweet dumpling.

"No problem darling, I can easily make sweet dumplings for the whole village."

At this, he nearly had a heart attack. "No, I won't allow it. The village doesn't need dumplings."

"Fine, then I'll just make some for our household," laughed his wife as she turned to leave.

But he caught her hand, "I don't want the servants to have any either."

Knowing her husband's miserly ways, she nodded, "Then I will just make some for our family."

Again he shook his head. "The children don't need any."

His wife sighed, "Very well I will just make two, one for you and one for me."

At this he sat up, "But why would you need one? I'm the one who is sick."

Though his wife was not happy, she made the dumpling which her husband quickly gobbled up.

It so happened that the god of heaven, Sakka, was watching the wealthy man and decided it was time to teach him a lesson. So the next day when the man went out for a walk, Sakka transformed himself into the man's likeness and went down to his house. There he told a servant to run to the village and tell everyone that he was opening up the doors of his treasure room to share all his wealth with the community. They could come and take whatever they wanted.

Pretty soon there was a stampede as the villagers clamored to get their hands on his gold and jewels. Wondering what all the commotion was about, the rich man followed everyone back to his house.

"Help, help, I'm being robbed," he shouted to anyone who would listen. The King, who'd heard about the free give-away, soon arrived to see for himself and heard the rich man's cries. "But your own servant told us, it was your wish to give your possessions away."

"That's nonsense," fumed the rich man, who had called for his wife to verify that he would never do anything so foolish.

When she arrived, Sakka, still disguised as the wealthy miser, was with her.

Shocked by the sight of his double, the rich man tried to explain. "Don't you see? He's an imposter!"

Not being able to tell who the real wealthy man was, the King asked if the wife could figure it out.

"I think so," she said, then asked the doubles, "Who is it better to be generous to - your neighbors or yourself?"

Sakka quickly replied, "It is best to be generous to all."

But the wealthy man stomped his foot indignantly, "This is a trick question. It is best to be generous to no one!"

The wife smiled to herself. It was quite obvious who her husband was, yet she had the chance at a new life with a generous man. "The first man is my husband," she lied.

The wealthy man was stunned. In just a few short hours, he'd lost everything - his home, his wealth and his family. Before the game could continue, Sakka revealed himself and explained that he had come to teach the man a lesson. "When you treat the world poorly, it will treat you poorly!"

In the West we have a saying for this too. "What goes around comes around." The Law of Correspondence helps us to understand that life is what you make it. If you want it to be wonderful, you will take steps to make it wonderful. However, in doing so, you must concentrate on the positives as opposed to the negatives. If you want a new flat screen TV, no amount of talking about how broken your old TV is will help bring a new TV into your life. The more you complain about how bad it is, the more you will dislike it. In fact, you're so concentrated on the old TV and so filled with contempt for it that you don't have time to come up with a plan to get a new TV. You haven't got the time because you are so busy letting everyone know how bad it is and how the very presence of it is ruining your life. The guy that sold you the old TV should be tried as a criminal for roping you into buying the thing, even if it was state-of-the-art 15 years ago when you bought it! He should have known better. He should have known that one day it wouldn't be new and you would no longer be pleased!

Ok, that illustration might be a bit silly, but you get the point. The Law of Correspondence helps us to understand that we create problems inside ourselves. Problems do not exist in the world. Things simply are! It is how we react to them and what we expect to happen or how we want someone else to act that creates the problem. The Meta Secret behind the Law of Correspondence is simple. Our minds create the beliefs that create the problems. At the core level, optimists and pessimists are the same. It is their beliefs that make them different!

"*Abundance and wealth are the keys to the Universe. They are the Universe. If you look around, there's nothing but the abundance everywhere. Trees growing, people enjoying themselves, business transactions taking place, this is wealth, this is prosperity, this is abundance.*

If it's not happening for you, it's because unconsciously you have beliefs, counter intentions, negativity that blocks abundance from coming into your life. The Law of Attraction is working all the time, but it's happening on an unconscious level.

The abundance is there, the wealth is there. If you don't feel it, if you're not expressing it, it's because inside of you, you may feel you don't deserve it. This is part of the unconscious work that must be done for you to feel on a conscious, Earth level what's happening with abundance and prosperity. Abundance, wealth is your natural birthright. If you're not feeling it, it's because of your unconscious beliefs."

Winston Churchill eloquently summarized this when he said, "A pessimist sees the difficulty in every opportunity; an optimist sees the opportunity in every difficulty."

This is a tough concept for many people to grasp. It would be so much easier if everyone else did as we asked. Wouldn't it be nice if our spouses magically appeared the moment we called their names, but could also sense in the split-second before they got annoying that they might be about to bother us and so they'd disappear? Our bosses would never have us do anything we didn't want and we could go to the store and take whatever we wanted - it would be nice right? My guess is the world would come to a standstill pretty quickly.

Though we logically understand that the world wouldn't last for very long if that were to happen, most of us haven't internalized that concept. We still believe that most of our problems are caused by *other* people, instead of understanding it is *our* perception that causes the problem! Because our ego tells us we have been insulted or in some way treated poorly, we begin to see situations as problems. In reality, whatever has just happened is most likely just fine with the other person, they do not see the situation as a problem or they would not have acted as they did. Such situations afford us the opportunity to construct our lives the way we see fit. We can begin to take responsibility for ourselves and understand that the only things we can control are our own thoughts and minds, or we can continue to blame everyone and everything else for our troubles.

Sometimes the easiest way to make changes in our own lives is to pretend that we are someone else who is very dear to us, such as a child, best friend, or spouse and then consider how we would advise them in our situation. For some reason, we are often more generous and protective of those we love than we are with ourselves and so, when we create our own allegory, we learn to treat ourselves with more kindness.

Then we can ask, "How are my actions in life, love, career and health being mirrored in the world around me?" "What do I need to do to start changing my world for the better?" Begin to visualize the changes and act in ways that will help them become a reality. In this way, through examining our 'blood', or the essence of our inner selves, the key to the world we desire becomes reality.

CHAPTER 4
Good Vibrations

Chapter 4
Good Vibrations

"Veni, vidi, vici," (I came, I saw, I conquered) Julius Caesar. "Ich bin ein Berliner," (I am a Berliner) John F. Kennedy. "One small step for man, one giant leap for mankind," Neil Armstrong. These historic quotes are powerful demonstrations of the third Hermetic law, the Law of Vibration. Not only do the sounds of these words create vibrations in the form of infamous words, but the feelings these phrases generate create vibrations as well.

I paused as I looked around at my audience to see if they were following what I was saying. All eyes were glued to me, the crowd respectfully silent as they waited to hear more. I smiled inwardly, realizing how far my journey had taken me. I'd become a psychotherapist and motivational speaker. I was sharing what I'd set out so long ago to do. Happiness vibrated through me as I continued my good vibrations lecture.

This third law says "Nothing Rests; Everything Moves; Everything Vibrates." That statement alone is pretty cool when you consider that it was written thousands of years before modern science, before anyone ever confirmed that the Earth's core vibrates at a frequency of 7.8 cycles per second, the same as the human body and long before we knew that all material substances, from rocks and trees to air and water, are composed of atoms, protons and neutrons, all of which are constantly vibrating.

According to the Law of Vibration, the ALL vibrates at a very high, steady rate while the three planes vibrate at increasingly slower rates. In other words, the only thing that divides the planes of existence is their vibrational frequency. So, as we briefly discussed in the last chapter, spiritual energy is faster than mental energy, which is faster than physical energy and each of these planes is divided into several increasingly lower speeds. On the physical plane, we can see this in the fact that humans vibrate at a quicker rate than a rock. However, if the rock were to pick up speed and begin to vibrate faster and faster with ever-increasing speed, it would eventually move up to a new plane of existence.

The Three Initiates explained the concept in this way: *When an atom vibrates fast enough, its molecules disintegrate and resolve themselves into the original atoms. Then the atoms, following the principle of vibration, are separated into the countless electrons and protons of which they are composed. With a high enough frequency of vibration, even these elements will eventually scatter. The remaining essence of the object is then composed of an ethereal substance. The faster vibrations liberate the object's light, heat and other energy from its previously confining molecules and atoms. If the vibrations were further increased, the dematerialized object would climb the successive mental and spiritual planes, until it would finally re-enter The ALL.*

While this all sounds very interesting in theory, few of us will probably live to see the day when we see blocks of pavement, chairs, or computer monitors begin to spontaneously rotate until they spin out of existence. To say the least, it just wouldn't be practical! However, the Law of Vibration does have a very practical application in daily life. Just as we all vibrate, each of our thoughts and emotions also vibrate. Some emotions, such as anger or frustration, vibrate at a much slower rate than other emotions, such as happiness and peace.

The Law of Vibration also connects back to the Law of Attraction. Each one of these emotional vibrations will attract a similar emotional vibration. We know this to be true because we see it in action all the time. What happens if someone pays you a sincere compliment? You feel good, right? And if someone starts screaming at you, chances are you'll yell back.

Such wisdom is extremely powerful because it can help you to shape your life and the lives of those around you. In psychology, there is something known as the Bystander Effect. In 1964, Kitty Genovese was brutally stabbed to death by a serial rapist and murderer. The attack went on for more than a half hour. During this time, newspaper accounts say at least 38 people witnessed the attack and murder and did nothing to help, not even call the police. Fear obviously played a role in this extreme case. But beyond that, it demonstrates that humans take their behavioural cues from each other, much of which is communicated through emotional vibration.

This transfer of vibration or feeling through emotion is known as induction. Gandhi and Martin Luther King, Jr., used it when they inspired and energized the masses to peacefully work for human rights issues. We often feel induction at sporting events, whether our team wins or loses. Induction plays a large role in wild celebrations in the streets, as well as when crowds turn and begin to riot and loot.

The Japanese believe the vibration of words rests within a spirit known as Kotodama. Because words can have such a powerful impact on our lives, a doctor named Masaru Emoto devised an experiment to try and physically measure emotional vibrations and see what they looked like. Because we are composed predominantly of water, he reasoned that one of the easiest ways to test his theories about emotional word vibrations would be to use water.

Dr. Emoto began taking pictures of frozen ice crystals which had been exposed to various forms of music. The water that 'listened' to Beethoven and Mozart formed beautiful, well-formed crystals, while the water that was exposed to heavy metal formed fragmented, broken or no crystals at all. Intrigued, Dr. Emoto continued his experiments, this time exchanging music for words. His results were similar. Bottles of water exposed to words with higher vibrations such as 'thank you' and 'gratitude' formed lovely, well-proportioned crystals, while water exposed to lower vibrational words such as 'stupid' and 'you fool' were fragmented or nearly non-existent. Curious, he decided to see what would happen if he tried other languages such as Chinese, English, French, German, Italian and Korean. Again, the results were the same; higher vibrational words consistently formed beautiful, 'healthy' crystals, while words of malice or hate produced the fragmented, 'sickly' crystals.

His conclusions were that words have a powerful effect on people; the high vibration of positive words has the ability to lift people up, while the low vibration of negative words has the power to destroy. Going back to the fact that we are all highly concentrated forms of water, you begin to see why words can have such a profound impact on us.

"In the beginning, there was the word.
I think the universe uses vibration to design words."

Dr. Emoto published his findings in his book *The Hidden Messages in Water,* which went on to become a New York Times Bestseller. In his book, he also employs the Law of Correspondence, saying that water mirrors the outside world! "We know what is possible in our hearts is possible. We make it possible by our will. What we imagine in our minds becomes our world. That's just one of the many things I have learned from water."

Just as crystal shatters when it is exposed to very high vibrations, or food in the microwave can catch on fire if exposed to too many vibrations, we too have our vibrational comfort zones. When we like something or it pleases us, we often will say it 'resonates' with us. We are attracted to certain smells, places and even people because they are in harmony with us or carry similar vibrations. Those we don't care for have different vibrational patterns from our own. The interesting thing about vibrations is that distance doesn't seem to have an effect on vibration. It makes no difference if you are ten miles or ten thousand miles from people or places that vibrate to your frequency because the laws of the Universe override distance. In fact, vibration in the form of radio waves is the key way in which scientists at the National Radio Astronomy Observatory in Green Bank, West Virginia, learn about outer space. Vibration may very well lead us to someday finding life on other planets!

Back here on Earth we're constantly surrounded by vibrations too. Besides words and emotions, we are exposed to the electronic vibrations of appliances such as refrigerators, lights, heating and air conditioning units, even our computers and cell phones. Because everything vibrates, everything makes a sound. Even if we can't hear it, we can feel it. Several studies from such groups as the Royal Institute of Technology in Sweden to the University of British Columbia in Canada have proven that the vibrations of such things as the low hum of office lighting or the low vibration drone of such things as computers, heating and cooling systems and water coolers actually lower workers' vibrations after prolonged exposure. This can lead to crankiness, low productivity and at times even workplace violence. Conversely, most of us have noticed how wonderful it feels to be outside on a beautiful day when the sun is shining and the birds are singing. These things are part of our vibrational code and so they resonate with us.

"As indicated in my earlier experiments, if words that do not resonate at the same frequency are put together, they become destructive energy that does not turn life into a beautiful form."

In 1989, scientist Warren Hamerman published an article in the journal *21st Century Science and Technology* that said organic material vibrates in a range 42 octaves above middle C on a piano. From this he was able to deduce that we all vibrate at approximately 570 trillion times per second. Furthermore, we appear to be the only animals that can resonate with all other animals and things in nature. Ancient Chinese tradition calls this resonating energy 'chi', while Indian traditions refer to it as the chakras.

One of the easiest ways we feel vibration is through music. Music is the only form of communication, i.e. human vibration, that can be universally understood without translation. The late singer and songwriter, John Denver, summarized it this way: *"Music does bring people together. It allows us to experience the same emotions. People everywhere are the same in heart and spirit. No matter what language we speak, what color we are, the form of our politics or the expression of our love and our faith, music proves: We are the same."*

Perhaps the main reason it can be understood so easily by anyone is that musical vibrations match emotional vibrations and so musical notes become emotional transporters. Have you ever felt a surge of pride when you hear your national anthem, or been moved to tears by a beautiful aria?

In fact, music is so powerful that back in the Middle Ages, the Catholic Church banned certain minor musical chords (which more recently have been proven to carry lower vibrations) as unlawful and dangerous, claiming it was the music of Satan.

Mothers have known for centuries that singing soothes their babies, while more recently music therapy has been used to help everything from frightened animals, such as skittish racehorses, to children with autism. Entrepreneurs know the benefit of soothing vibrations too. Why do you think so many restaurants and stores play relaxing music for their patrons? They know if they create positive vibrations, people will be willing to stay longer and spend more.

Enticing vibrations don't end with music; color is also made up of vibrations. Red has the shortest vibrational wave, while violet has the longest. So clubs might use red or black in their décor to build excitement among customers, while hospitals often use neutral colors to soothe patients.

Technically speaking, we can only see three one hundred-thousandth of the energy spectrum around us. If our eyes could detect more, we might be able to see the vibrations and colors of such things as gamma and x-rays, radio and satellite waves and ultraviolet and infrared light. What an interesting thought!

The Three Initiates believed that just as science has finally proven that the physical plane is made up of vibrational matter, some day science will also discover the same thing holds true on the mental and spiritual planes.

Science may be catching on to what ancient wisdom has always maintained. A study published in the October 25, 1999 issue of the *Archives of Internal Medicine* found that prayer (which is a form of spiritual vibration or energy) is just as effective whether people pray for those they know or strangers. Additionally, it didn't seem to matter if the patients knew they were being prayed for or not. More recently, The National Institute of Health has awarded several million dollars to researcher and doctor, Elizabeth Targ, to study the effects of prayer on AIDS and cancer patients. She has also researched distance healing (or spiritual vibration) with Christians, Buddhists, Jews and Indian shamans. Those prayed for had fewer repeat illnesses, fewer doctors visits, fewer hospitalizations and were generally in better spirits than the non-prayed for control group.

Because the Law of Vibration works by universal standards rather than physical laws, it may sometimes appear that it defies such things as space-time and gravity. But quantum physics has already proven how the Law of Vibration works on the higher mental and spiritual planes. (My apologies ahead of time to my physicist friends, who might be offended by such a simplistic explanation; however, my intention is to convey a general concept, so please excuse my brevity.) The way this was proven was with an experiment called the double slit test. In it scientists shot electrons one at a time at a screen with two slits, expecting that the electrons would pile up on the opposite side of the screen in the same pattern that they had been in on the first side of the screen. Instead the electrons formed a completely new pattern. Stranger yet, when the screen was removed weeks or even months after the experiment was complete, it changed the outcome of the already completed experiment! No matter how many times it was done, it always changed the outcome of an already completed experiment. This means that something that has already happened can be affected by a choice made at a later date - or a physical object can be in two places at once!

This experiment laid the foundation for understanding that quantum energy or vibrations which make up the way we think and act are not sensitive to time and space. They can affect our past or our future.

Dr. Valerie Hunt, an octogenarian and professor emeritus of physiological science at UCLA, has studied the human brain all her life. She says, "It is the mind which experiences and it is the brain which records the experience ... the brain can store memory, but it is the mind which makes decisions. The mind is independent and contains the will of humankind."

Therefore, she says that such things as imagination, creativity, intuition and spirit don't exist within brain matter, rather, they come from somewhere else. With as much as we've learned about the brain, we still can't really explain where altered states of consciousness come from.

She says these extra abilities help generate the vibrational field around us that carries one thousand to ten thousand greater frequencies of information per second than the neurological data we generate. Just like Dr. Emoto's ice crystals, Dr. Hunt says humans' energy fields give off coherent synchronized vibrations when they are healthy, but unbalanced vibrations when they are sick.

In Hunt's book *Mind Mastery Meditations,* she shows people how to use their energy or vibrations to deal with the pain of trauma, surgery and illness, saying, "The human mind is the greatest piece of equipment we have ever had and everything we have ever done in science since is a replication of what can happen in the human mind. So, when we doubt telepathy, knowing, intuition, we'd better drop it. This will be standard information in the future."

All this information about the Law of Vibration is really exciting because it means that we truly have the ability to make our world whatever we desire by raising our vibrations. We do that by taking a look at our emotions and understanding them. If something is making you feel bad, it is not in alignment with your vibration. The first step is to understand that you most likely can't change others or what they are doing, but you can change the way you perceive the situation. Realize that this is an incremental process, not a quick fix that takes you from 0 to 90 miles an hour in six seconds flat.

Take the example of missing a family member who's away on a trip. You may feel sad without them and can't jump immediately to being happy when they're gone, but think of something that may make you feel one step above sad. Maybe instead of thinking about the fact that they're gone, you can focus on the fact that every day that they're away brings you one day closer to their return. And so you're no longer sad, maybe just a bit blue. Then maybe you can focus on the fact that the time apart will give them a chance to really appreciate you and so you turn the blue to a feeling of neutrality. Life isn't great without them, but it's not too bad. You'll survive. Then maybe you can concentrate on the fact that they're growing, learning, perhaps even having a little fun while they're away. Perhaps you can do the same so that you have something interesting to tell them when they return and, besides, it would be a bit of a distraction to help keep your mind from pulling you back down. You plan a night out with friends and have a wonderful time. Before you know it, you are laughing and happy; time flies and your loved one returns!

So celebrate, put on some music that grooves to your vibration, surround yourself with colours that keep you happy, eat foods that are in harmony with your system. Every day is an opportunity to take steps to create a reality that matches your highest and best vibrations. As the Beach Boys said in their classic hit, it's all about 'drinking up good vibrations.'

CHAPTER 5

Everything Has An Opposite

CHAPTER 5
Everything Has An Opposite

The rain pelted down in large, icy drops, turning my usually sunny morning window into a smear of dark gray slate. As the storm raged outside, a Beatles tune poured from the portable radio on my desk. *"You say yes, I say no, You say stop and I say go, go, go, Oh, no, You say goodbye and I say hello…"* my fingers tapped along rhythmically as they moved across my laptop.

A streak of lightning ripped across the sky, illuminating my office before a sonic boom plunged the room into total darkness and silence. I waited in the luminescent glow of my computer screen for the lights to come back on. 'Thank goodness I was working on battery power or I could have lost everything,' I thought, as the minutes ticked by with no hint the electricity would be restored soon.

Since my 'aha' moment during my Good Vibrations Speech, it had occurred to me that my mission to find and share the Meta Secret was only half-complete. If I really wanted to share my experiences and knowledge with the world, I needed to write a book. I was literally humming with anticipation…the only problem was the Universe seemed to be conspiring against me. Or was it? I'd just said so myself, there really wasn't any reason I couldn't continue to work.

I lit a candle and began to type, "The Law of Polarity," then chuckled at the irony. Here I was about to explain the fourth law of the Universe and it was demonstrating itself all around me; rain and sun, light and dark, sound and silence, energy and stillness.

Of course those weren't the only examples of the law. The Law of Polarity is also sometimes called the Principle of Practicality. It says that all things are dual and everything has an opposite, which means opposites are identical in nature, only different in degree. The easiest example of this is an old mercury thermometer. Instead of looking at it as a thermometer, let's look at it as a pole of temperature. At one end of our pole we have icy cold measurements, while at the other end of our pole we have boiling hot measurements, in between we have varying degrees from cold to hot. If we start way down at zero, we know the temperature is going to be cold; however, eventually, as we move up our pole of temperature, things will start to become warmer and warmer until they begin to get really hot. Therefore, hot and cold are identical in nature because they both belong to the pole of temperature, they simply vary in degree. This works for everything - rich and poor, love and hate, near and far. Just think, if you started walking to your left and had the super power to walk through any obstacle and over water, you would eventually end right back in the same place you started!

"Recognizing the divine component in us has a two-fold effect. On the one hand it's incredibly humbling, because how many of us really live up to being Godly? How many of us really, really maximize our God-given talents? How many of us really live lives of fulfilled potential?

On the one hand, it's kind of intimidating but on the other hand it's very inspiring. It's inspiring to think - I as a human being, am capable of being Godly. I'm not God. I'm not going to confuse myself with God, but I am capable of being Godly. I am capable of a goodness which can resound around the world. I am capable, like God, of using language to bring things into existence."

The Law of Polarity is embodied in the yin and yang symbol. This symbol is chock-full of polarity: white and black, yin and yang and positive and negative. This symbol is especially interesting because it embodies so many of the universal laws. The yin and yang hold the essence of each other within themselves (the little dot of opposite colour within each swoosh) just as we learned that we are all part of each other in the Law of Mentalism. The symbol also touches on the Law of Vibration with the two symbols of yin and yang working in harmony to create a third new symbol for creation. This touches on our previous theme of three in one; physical, mental and spiritual, or the more divine theme of Father, Son and Holy Ghost; Earth, Heaven and Hell and on and on. The yin and yang also touches on a law we'll study in an upcoming chapter, known as the Law of Gender. Yin is female energy while yang is male in nature. Yang is seen as creative thought, while yin is the empty vessel of positive energy that attracts it. Both must work in harmony with each other to resonate and become reality.

There's an African proverb that demonstrates the concept of what happens if you do not learn how to reconcile the Law of Polarity. Once there was a very hungry hyena. It had been many days since he had eaten and so he could hardly believe his good luck when he came to a fork in the road and saw a goat trapped in the bushes at the end of each path. Like all hyenas, this hyena was an opportunist, but he took it to a whole new level. "Why should I go down one path," thought the hyena, "when I can go down both?" And so he placed his left two paws on the left path and his right two paws on the right path and began to walk. As the paths veered further and further apart he tried to follow them both until finally he snapped clean in two!

While the story teaches about greed, it also teaches us to work with the Law of Polarity, not against it, to achieve what we need or want. Because everything is composed of opposites, it means that no matter how big the issue we are facing, we can find the solution when we raise ourselves through the degrees of that particular pole.

The comfort within the Law of Polarity is that no matter how dark something seems to be the potential for light also exists. Therefore, while something may seem like a lost cause, a solution is always possible - it may not always be your first choice or what you expected, but there is something else out there.

The Three Initiates added the following wisdom to this law. *The positive pole is of a higher degree than the negative and readily dominates it. The tendency of nature is in the direction of the dominant activity of the positive pole. So you see that you can change your mental state by moving upward toward the positive pole and nature will help you along.*

The Law of Polarity is also seen as a paradox, because if everything has an opposite, then it could be said that everything is only a half-truth, yet because everything is a half-truth it can always be reconciled.

This also means that, no matter where you are within a current situation, you have the power to change your situation by raising your polarity to the positive end of the issue (or pole) that best suits your needs. The key to working with this law is to accept responsibility to move yourself to whatever pole degree you wish to be. The only thing that determines which way you will slide on that pole is your choice or set of choices. Therefore, while you may have all the required skills for a promotion, are you making choices that might help you secure that position, such as being friendly to co-workers or are you being condescending whenever the chance arises just to show that you are far smarter than anyone else at the office?

One of the most overlooked polarities when it comes to personal responsibility is acceptance. Acceptance is the opposite of resistance. It doesn't mean you should put up with poor treatment, stand for sub-par situations, or resign yourself to being *status quo* instead of striving for your potential. But accepting what you are experiencing is the opposite of resistance. If you accept the situation, you shift your pole a few degrees closer to the positive end of the situation. By the Law of Attraction, you will begin to draw that which you need into your life. Once you have accepted, you begin to find ways in which you can positively concentrate on the goal you wish to achieve, instead of placing your attention on the lack of having what you need or want. We did this in the last chapter with the example of missing a loved one.

Remember, concentrating on the negative lowers your pole position a few degrees each time you do it. Before you know it, you can make your situation ten times worse simply by thinking negative thoughts. Instead, try to catch yourself whenever you start to think the worst and replace that thought with one that is slightly better. This isn't about taking yourself to a level that you're not ready to go to, just one or two degrees above your current emotional state.

A great exercise to get people in the habit of thinking more positively is to play a game as you wait in traffic, stand in line, or whenever you find a little extra time on your hands. Observe your surroundings and begin to name as many things as you can which you like or find favorable. Stretch your imagination; there is something positive in every situation, even if it's just that the color of the walls remind you of your childhood blanket or the color of your grandmother's hair.

"Every choice, every moment, determines your life!"

Just like the Law of Vibration, the Law of Polarity is catching. You can begin to change the polarity of others by changing your polarity. How often has a compliment raised your spirits, or a rude comment brought you down? So choose to see the good in others and use it to your advantage. Be a little kinder, pay a compliment, smile. You'll be surprised how reciprocal such actions become. A few years ago, there was a movie about this very idea called *Pay It Forward*. Twelve-year old Trevor McKinney is intrigued by the classroom assignment in which Mr. Simonet asks his students to think of something that makes the world a better place and then implement it. Trevor decides to 'pay it forward' by doing three good deeds, not as repayment or payment for past favors, but simply to better the future. In turn, he believes that the recipients will do good deeds for others around them. What he initially believes to be a failure turns out to be a great success, when a reporter who is the benefactor of a good deed traces the 'pay it forward' project back to its roots.

Granted, I know the world is never as sunny as Hollywood makes it out to be. Life is seldom wrapped up in a pretty little package with a perfect bow. But it is a gift, nonetheless. I know that bad things do happen and people will behave in unfavourable ways, but by accepting that truth and then choosing to see the good, I begin to change *my* reality and draw positives back into my life.

"In order to achieve happiness in your life, you have to understand a few things: happiness and achieving happiness is a process. It's not something you achieve right now and you're done and you have you happiness. It's something that you're constantly attaining and re-attaining through life.

The way to do that is to really understand what brings contentment in your life and to achieve that. One of the key things to remember in terms of happiness is that part of this process is sharing happiness with other people. The more we share happiness and the more we teach other people how to bring happiness and fulfilment in their life, the more we'll be happier and fulfilled! So continue with your journey of greater fulfilment and you'll have more happiness in your life."

The Law of Polarity is catching on in the healthcare field as well. The National Institute of Health now recognizes a treatment known as Polarity Therapy to help patients with a variety of health issues through balancing the flow of various energy systems. The therapy was developed in the 1940s by Dr. Randolph Stone, who believed that a series of massage-like techniques would help clear the body of unbalanced, blocked, or fixed energy due to stress, which in part causes pain and disease. He based his new therapy in part on Ayurvedic medicine which concentrates on the chakras. To help a patient release their stress, the practitioner presses on opposite polarities within the body. Scientifically, it works with the electromagnetic long-line, transverse and spiral currents of the body.

Various treatments work with the physical, mental and emotional areas of the body. The therapy is named after the expanding and contracting action of energy as it moves away from the heart back to the heart.

A second aspect of the Law of Polarity has to do with the heart as well. It's the concept of gratitude. While it may look like the world might be a better place without certain polarities, would we really appreciate the kind sentiments of a loved one if we never encountered harsh words? While we might feel some gratitude, we probably would not understand the full extent of how precious a gift kind treatment is. If poverty did not exist, would we take wealth for granted or could we truly appreciate it? If we were immortal, would we comprehend how wonderful it is to be alive?

There is an urban legend attributed to Albert Einstein as a student. While it is just a legend and the esteemed physicist never took his professors to task in such a manner, it wonderfully illustrates the Law of Polarity:

"Did God create everything?" a professor challenged his class.

"Yes, of course he did," an athletic young man confidently responded.

"Really?" questioned the professor with a tilt of his head. "Well then," he shrugged as he paced back and forth in front of his lectern, "if that is true, by the principle at work here, if God created everything then he also created evil, because evil exists. This would in turn mean that God himself is evil if everything that exists is part of God."

Many of the students shifted uncomfortably, as the professor continued in an all-knowing voice. "You see, faith is just a myth, something the uneducated believe in to make themselves feel better. The learned accept the truth that God does not exist or there would be no evil."

"What?" asked the professor, a bit annoyed by a pretty blond in the first row, who was biting her lip and timidly raising her hand.

"May I ask a question?"

Loving to make a spectacle of the students he considered less intelligent, he nodded.

"Does cold exist?"

A chorus of giggles went up from the class. "Yes, of course it does," answered the professor feeling quite superior.

The young woman shook her head. "Actually it doesn't. Cold is only the absence of heat according to the laws of physics. All matter has the ability to transmit energy and heat is what makes that happen. However all matter becomes inert at absolute zero. Cold is simply the word we have created to explain the absence of all heat."

"Yes," agreed the professor not sure where she was going with this.

"Evil is the same as cold," she continued. "Evil doesn't exist by itself. It is something humans have created, a term we use when we feel the absence of God."

As a universal law, the Law of Polarity can't be escaped or tricked. It just is and so it will act without bias. By understanding both sides of poles we begin to develop a true appreciation and respect for the Law. The cool thing about this is that we can choose which degree of polarity we wish to set our lives to and work towards it.

As if to echo my words, rays of afternoon sunlight began to warm my keyboard. I looked up to find the sky painted in a fresh coat of robin's egg blue. "Yep," I smiled to myself, "polarity in action!"

Chapter 6
Go With The Flow

Chapter 6
Go With The Flow

Let's take a trip back in time. Big shoulder pads and skinny ties are in; miniskirts and mall hair are a must! The year is 1991. The first Gulf War is just getting underway, a new video game *Sonic the Hedgehog* has just been introduced to the world and the US Senate Committee on Aging is about to get a lesson in the fifth hermetic law, from Grateful Dead drummer Mickey Hart. Decked out in a tan suit jacket and pinstriped shirt, the percussionist looks every inch the diplomat instead of the world-famous rock star that he is. With more than 40 years musical experience, he begins to teach the committee about the Law of Rhythm and how it helps the elderly. The attentive audience quiets as he gently beats his hand on the desk in time as he explains:

"Everything that exists in time has a rhythm and a pattern. Our bodies are multi-dimensional rhythm machines with everything pulsing in synchrony, from the digesting activity of our intestines to the firing of neurons in the brain. Within the body, the main beat is laid down by the cardiovascular system, the heart and the lungs. The heart beats between sixty and eighty times per minute and the lungs fill and empty at about a quarter of that speed, all of which occurs at an unconscious level. As we age, however, these rhythms can fall out of synch. And then, suddenly, there is no more important or crucial issue than regaining that lost rhythm."

He tells the well-tailored politicians that rhythm can be seen in nature as well, in the migration of birds, the changing of the seasons, the cycle of life and death. Rhythm is the beat to which change moves forward through time. By understanding rhythm and working with the flow of it, we maintain mental, physical and spiritual well-being.

As he continues the lesson, I marvel at how seamlessly the Law of Rhythm ties the laws of Correspondence, Vibration and Polarity together - each needing the other, yet separate, ebbing and flowing with the grace of the Universe.

Ancient shamans were aware of this rhythm nearly thirty thousand years ago. Drumming is considered one of the oldest forms of healing. This bodily connection to rhythm has been practiced in every culture throughout the world. The simple, repetitive beats help the shaman to subtly change his patient's vibration by resonating with their physical, emotional and spiritual systems. Just as a tuning fork will cause stringed instruments to begin to vibrate at a specific frequency, the rhythmic beat of drums 'tunes' the body.

Science has now verified that the rhythm of many musical instruments' have therapeutic effects. Drums have been known to boost the immune system, as well as to provide relief for both Alzheimer's patients and children with autism. Similarly, harps have been shown to lower brain waves to the alpha state, relieving anxiety, depression and fear.

In 1994, music therapist Barry Bernstein co-founded a wellness program called "Unity with a Beat!" to help spread the word about rhythm and health. His corporate wellness program has been used by such big companies as Bayer Agricultural, Novus and Monsanto, Shell Oil Company and Sprint.

While the main objective behind these rhythm therapies is to promote physical health, many people are again listening to their inner rhythm and are being drawn to the primeval beat of drum circles for mental or spiritual reasons. As we learned earlier, vibration is the only thing that separates planes of existence. Therefore, drumming is a good way to raise your vibrations to higher levels of consciousness. As we also learned, group energy is contagious. Therefore, the positive interaction of a drumming circle can push individuals to new heights of awareness. In his book *Shamanism: The Neutral Ecology of Consciousness*, Michael Winkelman explains that drumming synchronizes the frontal and lower areas of the brain to blend non-verbal information and insight in a profound way that surpasses ordinary understanding.

Just as dogs can hear sounds far above the human range and radio frequencies invisibly bounce all around us, the Law of Rhythm constantly beats all around us in many unseen ways. It helps to explain why we have the swings we do with our emotions, feelings and moods. The Three Initiates described the process in the following way:

There is always an action and reaction, an advance and retreat and a rising and sinking manifested in all planes of the Universe. Suns, worlds, men, animals, plants, minerals, forces, energy, mind, matter and even Spirit manifest this principle. Rhythm manifests in the creation and destruction of worlds, in the rise and fall of nations, in the life history of all things and in the mental states of humans.

"If you are really secure in yourself and somebody criticizes you, it isn't going to bother you. However, if you are insecure and somebody criticizes you, it's really going to bother you. You see, about nine out of ten times, the person that is criticizing you really wants to help, they just haven't learned how to communicate effectively, rather than bringing out a couple of good points. If they're not doing it to help, then they're destructive. You don't want to be around those people anyway.

Let's not let somebody else's criticism or their way of helping us shake us. If we're solid in our own self and we really understand ourselves, then we can handle it and it won't be a problem. If criticism really rattles your chain, it's not the criticism that upsets you; it's not the other person's opinion that upsets you. It's how you react to it. If you're really solid within yourself, you wouldn't respond to it."

The Law of Polarity already taught us that emotional poles have two ends: the higher self - which knows what's best for us and can rise above the current situation, even when we're not so sure about the world - and the ego - which gets hurt and insulted, jumps to conclusions and generally ends up causing us trouble. Until we become fully aware of these two ends, our emotions are like pendulums swinging back and forth with no control. The Law of Rhythm says that we should expect to encounter these changes in our emotions because the first law of the Universe reminds us that life is always changing. However, we don't have to experience these swings as either being pampered by angels on a resort beach in Heaven or being dragged out to sea by a pack of rabid sharks. With some practice, you can steer clear of the sharks in times of trouble and instead gently float on the sea.

Finding this center of balance is sometimes called the principle of neutralization. Hermetists conditioned themselves to do this by refusing to slide back down whichever pole they found themselves in when things seemed to go wrong. They detached themselves from the situation and did not get pulled down by their egos, which might tip them towards feeling insulted, wounded beyond repair, or beaten into hibernation. They understood that it was all right to feel whatever feelings they had, but to let them flow through them, experience them and then let them go, so that they could move on.

Using the Law of Rhythm is a little like playing with a Chinese finger trap. Usually the owner entices an unsuspecting person to put one finger from each hand into the woven bamboo cylinder puzzle. The more the person tries to pull their fingers out, the tighter the trap becomes. The key to freeing themselves is to relax and go with the flow of the weave by moving their fingers towards each other. The more you fight feelings such as fear, anger and pain and the more you ignore them, the more difficult they become to release.

This is exactly what happened to the Hatfields and McCoys back in the late 19th century. The two families lived along the West Virginia/Kentucky border. Both were part of an early wave of settlers to the region and for a while, they got along. The Hatfields even hired several McCoys at their timbering company. But then the American Civil War broke out. The Hatfields fought for the South, while the McCoys fought for the North. Towards the end of the war, a McCoy soldier was murdered on his way home. The leader of the Hatfield clan was suspected of killing the McCoy boy. Later, it was proven that the accused Hatfield was home ill at the time of the murder, but by then there was no turning back. For 26 years the families fought each other, setting properties on fire, sabotaging each other's businesses, jumping lone rival members and even killing each other's wives and children. The event escalated into a bloodbath of such magnitude that the governors of both states called out their militias to put an end to the fight.

Yogis believe the Law of Rhythm manifests in the third chakra or solar plexus. Westerners who talk about a 'gut feeling' or feeling it in the 'pit of their stomach' are saying something similar. When we suppress our true feelings, they begin to fester and we develop resentments. We start to blame others with phrases like 'if you had only…' or 'it's all your fault that I…' Part of personal responsibility is to acknowledge that you are responsible for how you feel, no matter what anyone else does. No one else can 'make' you feel anything.

We've all met the person that refuses to acknowledge what they're really thinking. "What's the matter?" you might say. They'll respond, "Nothing, it's really nothing. Don't worry about it." However you know better because of the funny way they're holding their body or the twitch they've developed above their right eye. So you try again. "I'd really like to know.". "It's no big deal." By this time it's obvious that it's a very big deal. So you try again. "Please, just tell me." To which they reply, "I don't want to be a bother."

Or you may have met the type of people who just don't say anything and expect people to behave in a certain way or give them what they want.

No matter what the reason, whether you feel someone else should just know, you don't want to be a burden, you want to avoid a confrontation, etc., if you don't speak up and advocate for yourself, you are avoiding your personal responsibility to yourself. You're not doing anyone, any favors. It will not earn you brownie points down the road or help you become canonized as a saint. It is up to you to let people know what you're thinking or feeling.

It's also up to you to accept your feelings as normal and understand that in the rhythm of life everyone has highs and lows. If you're a little blue, don't feel like being social today at work, allow yourself a break. Be pleasant, but you don't have to be chatty. That allowance may take enough pressure off to move a degree or two up the emotion pole towards happiness. When you go with the flow, i.e. the Law of Rhythm, life becomes easier.

You don't swim against the current of a river, you try not to walk against the wind, so why would you work against the Law of Rhythm? The Meta Secret here is that using rhythm isn't about letting things happen to you; it's about being smart enough to allow yourself the leeway to move towards your goals. After all, we know that we bring into our lives that which we focus on. If we are focusing on going against the flow, how can we ever get where we want to go?

We can't solve our own nightmares in isolation, we must openly invite others in to hear our hopes and dreams. In this way we can help each other awaken to a more peaceful and happy reality.

Like the Law of Polarity, the Law of Rhythm reminds us that as the pendulum swings one direction it must compensate by swinging back equally in the other direction. A person who experiences great bitterness will also know great love. When the Hermetists practice neutralization, many people misunderstand this to be blunting the emotions so that the pendulum barely swings, instead staying centered towards the middle of emotional poles. To the contrary, as the Law of Polarity taught us, in order to gain a true appreciation for such gifts as happiness, love and peace, we must know their opposites. However, once we have experienced these things, we can detach ourselves by taking a step back when the pendulum swings in a direction we do not care for and remind ourselves that, very soon, it will be swinging in a more favourable direction. If we go with the flow, even when times look bleak we can accept that they're not what we hoped for and relax because the Law of Rhythm lets us know what will be coming.

"The key to abundance is to act in spite of fear.
Act in spite of doubt.
Act in spite of worry.
Act in spite of inconvenience.
Act in spite of uncertainty.
Act in spite of anything."

The Aborigines tell a story about using rhythm to find better times ahead. In the first times, there was a tribe of Aborigines that lived in the mountains. Their home was lush and plentiful, but to the West the land was flat, dry and barren and to the East there were more mountains and a treacherous climb. The people were worried because it had not rained in a very long time and their well was nearly dry. They would have to make a decision soon about moving from the beautiful place if it did not rain. But an elder comforted the people telling them to be positive, because things would soon change.

That night as the people slept, two greedy men decided to steal the last of the water supply. They put the water in an eelamun (eel-a-mun), a large vessel which they had to carry between the two of them.

When the rest of the people woke, they were very angry. But the elder cautioned them that their anger would not quench their thirst and challenged the people to change their circumstance. Soon a search party was organized to find the thieves.

Because the eelamun was heavy, the thieves left deep footprints in the earth, which made them easy to follow. Soon the search party caught up with the thieves. When the men saw their kinsmen coming to retrieve the water, they began to run. To stop them, the search party began throwing spears. One of the spears caught the side of the eelamun tearing a hole in it. However the thieves did not notice they were losing water as they ran. In a short time, the search party caught up with them. While they were discouraged to find so little water, they stayed positive because their elder told them something good would happen soon.

Now this was in the time of magic when strange things happened quite often. So as the men retraced their steps with the thieves, billabongs and waterholes began to spring up wherever water had dripped from the eelamun. Delighted with the abundant water supply, the men returned victorious to their village.

There the elders punished the thieves by turning one into the first emu and the other into the first blue-tongued lizard!

So how do you use the Law of Rhythm to your advantage? Instead of automatically judging others by jumping to conclusions, relax and take a step back from the situation. Perhaps that comment you took as an insult wasn't meant to be. Maybe there's a good reason why your friends weren't on time. Possibly they have a better way of doing something that might benefit you later. Letting go of our biases and giving time and space to many situations will provide explanations our egos did not consider. The Meta Secret helps us to understand that by releasing pettiness, blame and criticism and opening ourselves to the Law of Rhythm, we become more peaceful individuals. While it may be difficult to let go of these feelings we've let become habit, a Native American proverb puts most grievances into perspective. Ask yourself what your actions will bring in seven days, seven months, seven years and seven generations from now?

We can use this knowledge of the Law of Rhythm in our daily lives. Take for example a couple trying to conceive a child. We all understand that it's not a matter of getting pregnant one day and the baby arriving the next. This rhythm of life takes nine months, so the couple plans accordingly. They might start by preparing a room for the baby and buying supplies for her. Later, they might go to parenting or prenatal classes of some sort and then they might pick out names for the baby.

Similarly when it comes to starting a new business, we understand that it takes time to become profitable. Unless you are very lucky, you can't hang up your shingle and expect customers to flood to you. It will take time and hard work to grow. However, many entrepreneurs get impatient and try to force growth before it's time. This is similar to trying to bake a loaf of bread but opening the oven door every few minutes to see if it's ready yet. The same could be said of trying to grow a friendship or learning a new skill. There is a rhythm to life and trying to cheat it only cheats you.

Just as there is a rhythm to mastering the physical plane, mastering the mental and spiritual planes takes time too. Strengthening your inner self takes time. Getting to know who you are, what you want and how to interact with others to achieve that can't be a rushed job. But when we listen to our inner wisdom and quiet ourselves to hear the beating of our own hearts, we begin to understand the world as we never did before.

There's an Australian proverb that sums this up nicely. "We are all visitors to this time, this place. We are just passing through. Our purpose here is to observe, to learn, to grow, to love... and then we return home."

Or as Mickey Hart put it in his concluding remarks to the US Senate of Aging, "As a species, we love to play with rhythm. We deal with it every second of our lives, right to the end. When the rhythms stop, so do we."

CHAPTER 7

To Everything There Is A Season

CHAPTER 7
To Everything There Is A Season

Incense mingled with the musty smell of aged leather and long-forgotten secrets, as I wandered through the dimly lit catacombs of shelves in an ancient bookstore. I ran my hand over the faded labels, enjoying the experience but uncertain what I was looking for. As I neared the back of the labyrinth, my hand struck a large volume. Its edges were tattered and the gold leaf faded, but the size of the great book piqued my interest. In a cloud of dust, I coughed as I pulled the book to a footstool below.

As the air cleared, *The Wisdom of Euripides* peered up at me through the dwindling light. Intrigued, I gently opened the brittle yellow pages and began to read:

The best and safest thing is to keep a balance in your life, acknowledge the great powers around us and in us. If you can do that and live that way, you are really a wise man.

I smiled. What a beautiful way to begin an exploration of the Universal Law of Gender. Long ago, gender wasn't used specifically to differentiate between the sexes, but between types of things. The Latin root word for gender is 'genus'. Those who had to memorize classification systems in high school biology will remember that biologists use nine rankings to identify how closely living things are related to each other: life, domain, kingdom, phylum, class, order, family, genus and species.

So when we speak of the Law of Gender, we're talking about a 'kind, sort, or type' - which is actually closer to the modern French word 'genre' we often use, to describe categories of film and books.

The ancient Hermetists believed that every person, place and thing had both masculine and feminine attributes which worked together to form new creations. They saw masculine energy as external, something that was sent out into the Universe, while feminine energy was internal. Therefore, masculine and feminine energies worked together like a set of jumper cables. Masculine, which was positively charged, would constantly repel, while feminine or negative would constantly attract. Scientifically speaking, positive doesn't mean good and negative doesn't mean bad. They are just terms for the balance of energy flow. Hermes used feminine to describe the negative path of energy because it was a source of creation, just as women carry the new creations of life.

"Health! Not just physical health, not just eating the right things and getting exercise, but let's talk about emotional health and balance. This means doing what you love, loving what you do; looking forward each day, researching, helping other people, giving back. This is the Meta Secret to emotional health."

Therefore, the Law of Gender is a balancing system within every creation in the Universe. Many languages such as Spanish, Hebrew and Arabic, incorporate this approach to gender into their noun systems. Certain words are designated either feminine or masculine out of convention rather than an actual physical link to male or female attributes.

Hermetists took this further, breaking the human psyche into male and female energy forms. They likened the 'Me' energy, or the part of us that makes up our emotions, habits and moods, as feminine energy, while our 'I' energy - that which has wants and desires - as masculine energy. In other words Me is the creator and I is the doer. I is the aspect of being, while Me is the aspect of becoming. Each serves a purpose, yet neither could accomplish the task alone. (Psychology would later call this process self-theory.)

When we concentrate and work at it, we use both our Me and I to accomplish everything we do. The Me comes up with the idea; the I puts it into action. To use an example from the chapter on polarity, let's take the pole of happiness and sadness. Me would be the creator of your present mood, while I would be the force which works to move your current emotional level up or down the pole.

The Three Initiates explained this in great detail:

Since your mind created these feelings and other states, you can change them with your will. After learning to elevate your moods and outlook at will, you stop identifying with your mental states, emotions feelings, habits, qualities, characteristics and other personal mental belongings. You set aside the "not me" collection of curiosities and encumbrances. Clearly, this requires much mental concentration and power of mental analysis. Still, the task is possible for the advanced student and even those not so far advanced are able to see, in the imagination, how the process may be performed.

After this detachment process has been performed, you'll find yourself in conscious possession of a "self" which has 'I' and 'me' dual aspects: The "Me" is a mental womb that produces thoughts, ideas, emotions, feelings and other mental states. The Me reports to the consciousness with creative ideas and inspirations of all sorts and kinds. Its powers of creative energy are enormous, yet the Me must receive energy from its I companion to manifest its mental creations.

"It comes into really understanding something about ourself. We should start at a very early age and we should ask ourself, "Who am I?" You know, "What really makes me tick?", and get to know yourself. We're in a hurry to get a car, build a business, or buy a house. We should introduce ourself to ourself. School hasn't done it! Our parents aren't doing it. If you go to work for somebody, they're not going to do it. So if you don't do it for yourself you're not going to do it. This deal's between you and yourself. Pogo said "We've seen the enemy, they are us."

When we become aware of the Law of Gender, we realize just how often it occurs all around us. People in high-stress jobs are often unbalanced with too much masculine energy. When you constantly give in to competition, like many ladder-climbing young executives, work long hours out of need, such as many blue-collar workers, or have been taught to only think of others, as many mothers do, there is an energy imbalance. Just as a battery will stop functioning if only positive energy flows out of it, so will we. When everything around us is give, give, give, it wears away at us mentally, physically, spiritually and emotionally.

We were designed to have energy flow through us in both directions. Therefore, it is important to learn how to receive as well. We can do this by learning to accept help and receive gifts.

But just as too much male energy isn't healthy, neither is too much female energy. Those that wait for everything to be done for them or given to them, often become overly passive and no longer know how to act on their own or express original ideas. Instead of taking action to make their lives all that they can be, they slip into the role of victim.

When clergy instruct their congregations to act in a certain way, when an actor brings the audience to laughter or tears, when an activist incites a crowd to rally for a cause, they are all using their masculine energy or willpower to influence the feminine-accepting energies of their followers. The more you practice the balance of masculine and feminine energies, the less likely you will be influenced by the willpower (masculine energy) of others and the more control you will have over your thoughts, finances and freedom.

In addition to the concept of balance of masculine and feminine energy, the Law of Gender has a second meaning. Sometimes it is referred to as the Law of Gestation. It explains that it takes time to move seeds of thought to a fully functioning end result. The Haitians have a saying for this 'piti, piti, wazo fe nich li' or 'little by little the bird builds its nest'. Others might say, 'Rome wasn't built in a day' or 'to everything there is a season' - the point is that all thought and action require a period of incubation. For instance, we know that the Earth spins around the sun every 365 days, babies are typically born after 9 months and zinnias will sprout within 6 days of planting.

However, for whatever reason, whether it be the Information Age, a sense of entitlement or anything else, we have become a society that wants everything now. We fail to work with the rhythm of the Earth and recognize its cycles.

The difference between our setting goals and working to achieve them and such things as the Earth's journey around the sun, or the planting of zinnias, is that the deadlines or dates are not as easily recognizable. Sometimes we have to accept that not knowing the exact timing is part of the process, but that just like that flower that knows when to appear, goals will manifest when the time is right.

In the 1984 classic movie, *The Karate Kid*, Daniel Larusso asks handyman Mr. Miyagi to teach him karate. The handyman agrees and invites Daniel to his house where he puts the teen to work waxing his car, painting his fence and doing various other chores. Daniel puts up with it for a while before exploding and accusing Mr. Miyagi of taking advantage of him. It's only then that he learns Mr. Miyagi has been preparing him by naturally teaching his body the moves he will need to become stellar in karate. What Daniel did not understand is that karate wasn't about learning a few quick moves to take down an opponent, it was about truly learning the sport, the philosophy and becoming one with it. In the same way, we need to understand that life doesn't happen automatically and we often need to take time to learn and enjoy its nuances to truly benefit.

Part of reaching a goal is to have persistence and faith. As Wallace Wattles, the author of one of the earliest books on Hermetic laws once wrote, "The grateful mind continually expects good things and expectation becomes faith." Through the Law of Attraction, we know that having faith brings your goals to you. Your goals will come to fruition when the time is right.

The problem is that often times we say we have faith in something and we give it some effort, but at some level we really aren't clear with our intentions and so we often sabotage ourselves by not following through. For instance, if we decided to walk to the local ice-cream parlor, the best way to do it would be to walk out of the house, down the street and follow the general route to the ice-cream parlor on Main Street. We wouldn't walk out of the house, start walking towards Main Street, then decide to circle a block somewhere along the way three or four times, walk another block, then walk two blocks away from Main Street, realize we had wasted too much time and head home. Yet that's what we often do when it comes to believing in our goals. Instead of walking directly to the ice-cream parlor, we take a very meandering path, which often makes things take much longer than necessary or defeats the mission altogether.

If goals aren't coming to you as fast as you believe they should and you still believe in their worth, be confident and don't give up. Know that it will happen. Sometimes you just need to change your deadline.

You don't take diet pills and give up if the weight doesn't come off within seconds of swallowing them. You don't take one dose of penicillin and wonder why your throat infection isn't cured, so don't give up when the going gets tough, relax and know that everything happens in its own time.

Believe that what you have asked for is already coming to you - cultivate that faith. If you believe in it, know that you already have it; it is only a matter of time. If faith seems too difficult, remember the step up suggestion from earlier and begin moving towards that which you desire by degrees. Begin with appreciation and gratitude for that which you already have and work your way up to faith and belief. Goals always manifest when the time is right. That is the law of the Universe and it cannot fail. You may misunderstand the process or not see the whole picture, but eventually it will all become clear.

"Humor is good, it really is. I don't really understand what it does to you, but I know it does something to your brain. Norman Cousins, who is gone now, lived a long and very, very effective life. He'd been diagnosed with a terminal disease. He was literally dying. One day he got thinking to himself, "If sadness and sickness are hooked together, then happiness and health must be hooked together." And so he had people bring in old movie films of Laurel and Hardy and all kinds of different old, old actors, funny, funny stories. And he started to play them and laughed. They made him move out of the hospital. So he rented a suite of rooms in a hotel and he had these movies playing all the time.

And he got better. Now I think you know when you are laughing you are feeling good. Start to laugh at yourself. When you make a mistake, laugh at yourself. Don't get serious with yourself! It plays a very, very important role in a healthy relaxed life. Do you want to study it further? Get into some of Norman Cousins material. He'll explain exactly what it does to the brain that controls the vibration of the body. Start laughing a little more. Have fun!"

Motivational speaker Dan Millman shed some light on the process when he explained it in the following way: "I learned that we can do anything, but we can't do everything. At least not at the same time. So think of your priorities not in terms of what activities you do, but *when* you do them. Timing is everything!

As I closed the ancient dusty text, I marveled again at how well the laws of the Universe worked. I had walked into the old bookshop not knowing exactly what I would find and had been schooled in the ever-present Meta Secret flowing all around us. In this case, my search for a way to explain the Law of Gender had acted itself out before me.

It reminded me that instead of saying 'This will never work' or 'It's just not going to happen,' which kills the positive energy of faith, male energy can be used to redirect yourself to a more positive line of thought. You don't need to concentrate on how it's going to happen or when, or that it doesn't seem possible; by thinking it and sticking to that faith, you have already created. It will come, it is just a matter of timing. Are you prepared to wait?

By understanding the laws of the Universe and aligning yourself with them, everything will come to you in good time. It's just a matter of patience and keeping your eyes open to the possibilities!

CHAPTER 8

Nothing Happens By Chance

CHAPTER 8
Nothing Happens By Chance

Darkness filled the air as we struggled onward through the thick jungle vegetation. Our earlier decision to push forward into the night seemed of little consequence at the time. We were young and healthy; nothing, not even pitch-black darkness, could stop us! Something in the back of my mind whispered that I had done this before, but I brushed the voice aside.

My clothes clung uncomfortably to me in the humidity. The sweat that beaded my brow kept trickling down into my eyes making my trek all the more difficult. As I reached to wipe my eyes, I lost my footing and plummeted off the steep slope.

My heart raced as I flailed desperately, trying to break my fall. Momentum beyond my control hurtled me forward as I was flung about like a limp rag doll. It was happening again and there was nothing I could do to stop it. I remained suspended for an eternity somersaulting over and over with dizzying speed. I knew what was coming next. *'Don't use your hands. Don't use your hands to catch yourself this time,' I frantically instructed myself. 'If you do,' argued my mind, 'things could be a lot worse. You might hurt your head and become brain-damaged or even die.'*

I awoke with a body-slamming jolt as I hit the floor of the grotto. The bad dream was suddenly over. Life was safe again.

Scientists have known for a long time that dreaming is one of the ways in which humans process the hermetic Law of Cause and Effect. We use this dreamtime, free of ego, to subconsciously review situations so that we can either come to terms with our past actions, or prepare to take action should a specific event arise. Scientist Matt

Walker at Harvard Medical School has even used fMRIs (functional magnetic resonance imaging) to prove that the dream cycle literally restructures the neural representation of memory. That means that evaluating cause and effects, whether they have previously occurred or have the potential to occur, is a built-in instinct.

The Law of Cause and Effect is one of the best-known laws of the Universe. Many of us have studied this in science class as in 'for every action there is an equal and opposite reaction'. We understand that in order for any effect to be seen, felt, smelled, tasted, or heard, something - a cause - must have existed first. Apple pies don't bake themselves, babies don't just appear and this book didn't manifest itself. Something happened in all these instances which led to the pie, the baby and the book.

Because the Law of Cause and Effect is so ingrained within us, we often take it for granted. Yet, if you've ever had a conversation with a small child, you'll find they're very good at reminding us.

"Why are you putting training wheels on my bike?" asks Kaleb.
"Because," responds his father, "they will keep you safe while you ride your bike, so you don't fall over."
"But why will I fall over?" asks the child.
"Because gravity will make you fall," responds his father.

Kaleb looks around for this gravity character and doesn't see him. The coast must be clear for now so he continues his questioning. "But Cameron rides without training wheels. Why doesn't gravity get him?"

"Well at first it did, but now your brother has learned to balance."
Kaleb thinks for a moment, "But how did he learn to do it?"
"By using the training wheels," replies his father.

Any adult with a three or four year old has had several of these cyclical conversations. Learning cause and effect is one of the ways in which we come to understand the world and how we need to react within it.

Perhaps that is why so many stories from *Beauty and the Beast* to *Peter Rabbit* to *The Cat in the Hat* are so popular; they teach us about cause and effect. While we may overlook cause and effect as we grow older, the universal law is always with us, from cramming for a big test to not voting, from keeping pets to deciding to have children, from listening to your parents to not following your boss's instructions, from running away to coming home and on and on. No matter where we are, there it is.

Religious writings remind us of the universal law too. The Bible opens with a cause, "In the beginning God created the Heavens and the Earth." The rest of the book deals with the effect of creating these places.

Similarly the *Shvetashvatara Upanishad*, a sacred Hindu text, explores the Law of Cause and Effect:

> *What is the cause of the cosmos? Is it Brahman?*
> *From where do we come? By what do we live?*
> *Where shall we find peace at last?*
>
> *What power governs the duality*
> *Of pleasure and pain by which we are driven?*
>
> *Time, nature, necessity, accident,*
> *Elements, energy, intelligence--*
> *None of these can be the First Cause.*
> *They are effects, whose only purpose is*
> *To help the self rise above pleasure and pain.*

Buddhist, Jain, Sikh and Hindu religions adhere to the concept of cause and effect when they speak of karma. Karma simply means to act or do a deed. In western terms we might say 'you reap what you sow'. Famed Swami Maheshwarananda says we produce karma in four ways: through our thoughts, our words, the actions we do of our own will, the actions we perform on behalf of others. Conscious actions bear more weight than unconscious actions, but just as a smoldering match can start a fire whether you realized it was not out before tossing it, karma will always catch up with you.

"That original blueprint is a combination of different vibrations that are in balance with each other. If the blueprint falls apart due to some factors, we build up stress and finally become ill in the end."

An ancient Chinese discipline of cause and effect known as Feng Shui (pronounced 'fung schway') involves the art and science of inviting energy known as Ch'i (pronounced 'chee') into a space, such as a home, garden, or business, to improve the user's life or destiny.

It centers on the idea that balancing the energy of a living or working space will harmonize the people who live or work within the area. By working in harmony with this life energy, inhabitants of the space use the Law of Attraction to draw what they want into their lives.

Mega corporations like FedEx, Fuji Film, Intel and Nike all use Feng Shui in their corporate offices. Even more conservative companies such as Eli Lilly, Hyatt and Shell manipulate their corporate environments with Feng Shui to create harmony in the workplace, while business super-moguls Donald Trump, Bill Gates and Richard Branson are also fans of the ancient cause and effect philosophy.

Trump in particular has been known to spend a small fortune to make sure Trump Tower contains the right energy. Using the principles of Feng Shui, he instructed that the main entrance be built facing Central Park to allow the positive ch'i of prosperity to flow into his building. To keep the negative energy of the traffic from rushing at the building, a giant globe was placed in front of the building to block bad energy.

In addition to physically changing the energy of a space, Feng Shui teaches that people are in control of their own destinies through their actions. Physically placing a mirror in an area to bounce positive energy throughout a structure is one thing; however, it will never help if the user continues to act in negative ways. In this way, the Law of Cause and Effect helps people to understand that personal responsibility is necessary in all situations. If you have been raised to believe that 'money is the root of all evil,' it's very unlikely that you will attract money into your life. You don't want 'evil' in your life so consciously or subconsciously you will avoid money. You won't apply for profitable jobs, won't buy lottery tickets and will shun expensive clothes, meals and trips. However, if you begin to see money as neutral energy, just as water is energy or wind is energy, it quickly becomes clear that it is how that energy is used that can be helpful or destructive. It is how we use things that give them cause and effect.

Therefore, whatever we think must draw to it something of equal intensity because like vibrations attract like vibrations. Our thoughts cause, generate and grow whatever actions come back to us, in other words, the effect. Latin Americans have a humorous and visually descriptive way of illustrating the concept. They say 'El que escupe al cielo en la cara le cae,' which means 'He who spits up into the sky will have spit fall upon his face!' Australians simply call it the boomerang effect!

"The Meta Secret to relationships is to be the person you're looking for, Whatever it is you're out there looking for, be that and give it away. If you're looking for someone who is loving, kind and compassionate and generous, you need to be loving, kind and compassionate and generous. Whatever it is you want, you've got to be that and express that out into the Universe. Whatever you express out is going to come back multiplied."

The Law of Cause and Effect works similarly to gravity. No one is sitting in judgment of you for misdeeds and doling out punishment. It is much simpler than that. When you take action, it will draw to you a reaction.

Therefore, when my friends and I decided to press on through the treacherous jungle, we set the cause for a chain of events which led to my fall. I never cursed gravity for 'making' me fall. My actions led to the fall. No matter how difficult it might have been, I could have said to the others in my group that we needed to make camp and stay put. If they had refused, I could have made the choice to stay alone. That could have led to other difficulties, such as getting lost or being left to defend myself against wild animals, but nonetheless the personal responsibility of cause rested with me. It never occurred to me to blame gravity, just as it never occurred to me to blame the Law of Cause and Effect, because these are universal laws that exist without bias. We know that's just the way things are. So, no amount of arguing will change them and there's no point to arguing - it won't change the operation of the laws. They just are!

However, that's exactly what we do when things don't go our way. It was the weather that made me crash - not the fact that I decided to take the car out in 85 mile an hour winds with blinding snow. It's my husband's fault that I'm angry with him, he should know better - not the fact that I never told him what I really thought about buying a puppy for the kids. It's that ugly, little man at work's fault that I got fired - never mind that I treated him poorly for the last three years and he'd finally had enough of my abuse.

Long, long ago in the Republic of Surinam, a small country in South America, there was a huge forest fire, which helped the people to understand the importance of personal responsibility within the Law of Cause and Effect. Nearly all the animals died in the fire, but the snake hid deep in his hole and waited it out. The raging blaze came to an end when a heavy rainstorm swept through. But the water made the ground so soggy that the snake couldn't climb out of his hole.

"Help, help," he screamed until his lungs were sore, but no one could hear him. The snake had nearly given up when a young man happened by the hole. "Please help me," croaked the snake.

The young man wasn't sure what to do. After all, he knew the snake's disposition and was certain the snake would bite him.

"I promise I won't," whispered the snake, who'd nearly lost his voice.

And so the young man pulled him out. But as soon as he did, the snake tried to take a big bite out of him. "No, you shouldn't harm those who help you."

"How do I know others act this way?" asked the snake.

"Come with me and I will prove it to you," said the young man. "If I am wrong you can bite me."

A little way down the road they met a horse and asked him if evil should be returned for a kind deed. The horse snorted, "Of course! I am constantly whipped for my hauling services."

The snake laughed, delighted, "You see, I told you so."

Not convinced, the young man would not allow the snake to bite him. In a short while they crossed paths with a cow and asked the same question.

The cow casually chewed her cud as she answered with conviction, "I fully expect to be butchered for giving milk."

The snake got ready to claim his prize, when a wise woman happened upon them. "What's this?" she asked. When the pair explained to her what had happened, she asked if they would take her back to the hole, so she could better understand the situation. At the hole she encouraged them, "Please show me where you both were." So the young man helped the snake back into the hole and began to call for help again. But before the young man could help the snake out a second time, the wise woman stopped him.

"I believe I have the answer," she told the two. "The snake must get out of the hole on his own so that he will come to appreciate a kind deed. Until he does he will never understand!"

The Law of Cause and Effect helps us to understand that nothing happens by chance. If we can't find the cause, it doesn't mean there isn't one, it means we are not aware of it or can't identify it. Everything happens for a reason and that thing we believe we shouldn't have done contains a valuable lesson that helps us to grow in some way, or triggers an effect that may never have otherwise happened down the road. Perhaps you have been fired. While being let go is a horrible feeling, maybe it spurs you to start your own business that you never would have had the confidence to do, had you stayed in your secure yet frustrating old job. Maybe that break up with a long time girlfriend leads to meeting and marrying a soul mate you would never have known if you'd stayed with the less compatible yet comfortable old relationship.

The important thing to understand about the Law of Cause and Effect is that causes don't create the event; they are the impetus in a long chain of behaviors and beliefs. If you come from a heavy family where everyone one around you is heavy, you may hold the belief that your family simply has 'fat genes' and therefore you will never be thin. While you may never be a super model or a toothpick, there is a good chance you could be slimmer and healthier. However, if you believe nothing can be done about the situation, you won't work to improve it. It's not important to trace every effect to its initial cause. In the cause of the overweight family, it may have been going on for generations and there may be no way to ever identify the root of it. What is important is to be aware that everything has a cause and effect and to align your intentions and acts to correspond with the outcomes you wish to achieve.

"If you're looking for love and not finding it, it's no doubt because of a lack of forgiveness in some area of your life. This is true for all of us. You want to look in your life, look at your past, look at all your relationships and ask yourself, "Where have I not forgiven?

Is it myself, my parents, my siblings, my neighbors, my relatives, my business partners, where have I not forgiven?" When you go and forgive, you release the energy that allows the Law of Attraction to bring new love and new relationships into your life.

How do you do this? You ask yourself, "Where have I not forgiven?" and somebody will come to mind. It could be you! The second thing you do is say, "Can I forgive them? Can I forgive myself?"

Whether you say 'yes' or 'no', you move on and ask what made that person act the way they did at that point. "What made me act the way I did at that point?" And you start to go deep into understanding the psychology of behaviour. You realize we're all doing the best we can, yourself included.

When you forgive them, you release all of the energy that stuck psychically within your own mind and your body and your soul. And when that releases into the universe, the universe now has an open pathway to return to you new love, new relationships, new blessings. It all begins with forgiveness and you can do that, right now!"

As our friends The Three Initiates put it:

Some people are slaves to their heredity and environment and enjoy very little freedom. They are swayed by the opinions, thoughts and customs of the outside world and also by their emotions, feelings and moods. They claim that they are free to do whatever they want to, without analyzing the reasons why they want to do something.

Too many people are carried along like the falling stone, obedient to environment, outside influences, internal moods and the desires and wills of others stronger than themselves. Moved like the pawns on the checkerboard of life, they play their parts and are laid aside after the game is over.

The best way to start working with the Law of Cause and Effect is to notice your thoughts throughout the day and be aware of which thoughts are well formed to help improve your life and move you in the direction you wish to go and which thoughts just pop into your head, but don't serve any benefit. Be gentle with yourself and know that it will take practice to encourage the positive thoughts and actions. When the unnecessary thoughts pop in, simply let them pass through and get back on track with the productive thoughts. It will take some time, but with a little practice it will become easier and easier.

Part Two

Most people are uncertain about something. They're uncertain about their next step.

Here's the Meta Secret – Do it! Do it! Whatever you're uncertain about, do it!

Take the step. You will learn so much more! You will get so much further faster by actually getting in the game and doing it than thinking about it forever.

What I'm saying is one step in the right direction is worth a hundred years of thinking about it.

Chapter 9
The Simplicity Of Synchronicity

CHAPTER 9
The Simplicity Of Synchronicity

As I sat at my desk researching an appropriate symbol for the cover of *The Meta Secret*, my new assistant scooped the Ehwaz rune from the place where I always kept it. "What's this?" he asked me as he turned it round and round, trying to guess which direction it was supposed to face.

> I absent-mindedly glanced at him. "That is a symbol of my life's journey."
> "Hmm," he mused, "I thought it had something to do with your book."
> "My book, why?"

He rotated the rune one more and set it in front of me. "Because, it looks like an 'M' for Meta Secret."

A chill of delight ran down my spine. That was it! It had been with me all these years and though it was important to me, I had never connected it to my present work. But then again, that's the way synchronicity and the Law of Attraction work. When you give yourself the freedom to relax and just go with the flow, they'll show up every time.

Carl Jung, the famous Swiss psychologist, coined the term synchronicity back in the 1920s. According to Wikipedia, it is "the experience of two or more events that are causally unrelated occurring together in a meaningful manner. To count as synchronicity, the accounts should be unlikely to occur together by chance."

While the dictionary tells us they are unrelated, the laws of the Universe help us to understand that, nothing is by chance. Everything has an opposite pole, a connection, a cause and effect. Therefore, there is a link even if we can't pinpoint it. The question is, what do these events mean and how can we benefit from them?

The answer is to quiet ourselves enough to listen to the rhythms of the Universe and realize that there is more at work even if we are unaware of the forces behind that which we experience.

One of the ways that we can use the laws of the Universe on a daily basis come through 21 sub-laws. We have heard about them all our lives, but seldom stop to recognize their true power. They are: aspiration to a higher power, charity, compassion, courage, dedication, faith, forgiveness, generosity, grace, honesty, hope, joy, kindness, leadership, non-interference, patience, praise, responsibility, self-love, thankfulness and unconditional love.

We have already touched on many of these as we learned about the seven universal laws. In the coming chapters, I will explain how we can better use these attributes and what powerful gifts they are. While that may seem clichéd, I promise you it is not - because when we think in a certain way, it follows that we will act in that way, thus drawing that energy to us. All it takes is a slight shift in thought.

The Hopi Indians of the American Southwest have a tradition that helps them shift their thoughts to overcome disappointment. Every day they pray to the Great Spirit to allow them to make twenty mistakes. Their philosophy is that we can always learn from our mistakes, errors and failures. So, the more we mess up, the better we become because we have learned from the experience.

By shifting the focus of their attention to a more positive perspective, they not only become happier and healthier individuals, they also align themselves with universal law and begin to attract that which they want to themselves. While such philosophy goes against traditional education systems which teach that failure is not an option, adopting a positive attitude and following the laws of the Universe will reduce stress and heartache in any family, group, or organization.

This reminds me of another Meta Secret that I have shared once before in my earlier book, *Uncommon Sense*. In it, I explain that there are several ways of thinking - that we're often not aware of that become our undoing. I call it the *Twelve Beliefs That Will Cause Problems!* After all these years, they still hold true and so I'm re-printing them for you with a few tweaks I have learned after implementing my own advice!

1. EVERYBODY MUST LOVE ME!

This is the idea that we constantly need love and approval from others. Sometimes when we don't get the attention we feel we deserve we begin to feel inadequate. If it goes on long enough, we develop serious problems. But as we have learned with the Meta Secret, the more negative energy we put out there, the more we will draw to ourselves. We have the ability to control whether we keep our spirits high and remain at the set point we have designated for ourselves on the pole of love and hate or whether we let ourselves slide down the pole to more negative feelings.

The most important thing to remember is that we don't need to have the love and approval of everyone else, as long as we love and approve of ourselves. After all, we don't like or approve of everyone we meet, so why should we expect more of others than we do from ourselves? We all have freewill, so it would not be fair to take people's right to choose their feelings away from them, anymore than it would be alright for someone else to take away our right to like or not like others.

2. I Must Be Good At Everything!

This is the concept that we must do everything well in order to have value and feel good about ourselves. Sometimes we have to give ourselves permission to fail. Remember the Hopi philosophy we just discussed? Not being good at everything gives us the ability to grow and learn from our mistakes, which will make us better people. Concentrating on fear of failure will often keep us from doing a good job.

The Meta Secret reminds us of so many things when it comes to this mistaken belief such as: everything happens in its own time for a reason and the world becomes balanced when we are allowed to excel at our own talents and we allow others to excel at theirs.

3. Some People Are Bad: They Must Be Punished!

It's sometimes difficult to understand that just because someone takes a different standpoint than you, it does not mean they are 'bad.' The Meta Secret teaches us through the Law of Polarity that there is no such thing as 'good' and 'bad', only degrees of difference. Actions in and of themselves are simply energy. It is the way we interpret them that makes us feel they are positive or negative. The only thing we can do about any situation is to change ourselves. Sometimes that means slightly adjusting a belief, other times it means walking away from a situation or person.

I don't want others to control my actions, thoughts and beliefs any more than they want me to control theirs. We all deserve respect and decent treatment.

4. Things Should Be Different!

We can learn from the past and prepare for the future, but we live in the moment. Therefore, lamenting over your current situation and pointing fingers at others or even fate for what has already happened will do little to change it.

There is no reason to get upset if things aren't exactly the way I want them to be. I do not control the world and it is not my job to control it. My only job is to take personal responsibility for myself and to manage my life and actions.

5. It's Your Fault I Feel This Way!

No one can make us feel anything we don't want to feel. Our egos may react to what someone else has said or done, but it is not up to them to please us. It is alright to feel however we want to feel, but we must recognize that that is our reaction to an outside event. Instead we need to allow our feelings to flow through us, ask our inner guidance system why we are feeling the way we do and then let those feelings go and take steps to bring the situation into better balance.

6. I Know Something Bad Will Happen Soon!

This is the belief that we need to always watch for things to go wrong. "A car may hit me. A dog may bite me. A lion may eat me on the way to school. I must worry about it so I can be ready for it. I must keep watching; I can't relax."

Most of the time, things are just fine. In fact, we live most of our lives in a state of 'OKness'. We are clean, dry, well-fed, relatively healthy, not too hot or cold etc. Worrying that things will go wrong is a waste of energy. The Meta Secret tells us that because life is constantly changing, few things will go down exactly as we expect them to - so no amount of worrying will prevent a situation from taking place, if it is meant to. In fact, by the very act of worrying about something, we may actually draw that thing to us!

7. It's Easier Not To Even Try!

We sometimes refer to this mistaken belief as defeatism. It's the concept that it's just easier to avoid difficult tasks than to face them. In some cases we might use this belief because we are lazy. In other cases, we may simply not take on the responsibility that comes with reaching a goal.

The book *Think and Grow Rich*, by Napoleon Hill says that the reason more people do not succeed is because they fall victim to this false belief. The book explains that the one overwhelming characteristic that successful people such as Henry Ford, Alexander Graham Bell and others had in common was the ability to persevere even through tough times.

8. I Need Someone Stronger Than Me!

The Meta Secret tells us that because the Universe is one, everything we need is already inside us. While we may not be physically able to do some things - such as carry a sofa up a flight of stairs, we do have the ability to ask for help. If we can't find a friend to help, we always have the ability to think and come up with a new solution: maybe we hire a crane to hoist it up through a window, maybe we store it somewhere else for a while, maybe we sell it.

We must learn that while it is sometimes nice to have the help of another person, everything we need is already inside ourselves. We are completely capable of taking care of ourselves and making our own decisions.

9. I Can't Help Being This Way!

This is the idea that we are who we are because of our past and nothing will ever change the way we behave - that our lives are set in stone and that's just the way it is. Every day is a new day and therefore a new opportunity to change for the better.

10. I Should Get Upset About Your Problems!

We sometimes mistake solving other people's problems for love and support. We think that in order to help them we need to show them that their problems are our problems. In fact, this is not true.

Everyone must learn from their own problems. We can listen, offer suggestions and help from time to time, but it is up to them to take care of themselves, just as it is up to us to take care of ourselves.

By doing everything for another person we deny them the opportunity to learn, grow and reach their full potential.

11. THERE IS ONLY ONE GOOD WAY TO DO IT!

The Meta Secret here is that there is always another way to accomplish your goal. Some ways may work better than others, but because the Universe is mental, the number of possibilities when it comes to performing a task are only as limited as the imaginations of those working on it. I have a friend who often jokes 'There's more than one way to skin a cat' (which refers to cleaning a catfish, not making fur coats out of the family pet) and she's right. Whatever you can imagine, the Universe will bring to you. What a wonderful world!

12. I FEEL THIS WAY SO IT MUST BE TRUE!

This is when you say to yourself, "I feel guilty. Therefore, I must have done something bad." It's an example sometimes of how your emotions seem to be evidence for the thought that you were thinking. It rarely occurs to a depressed person to actually challenge this pattern of distorted thinking or reasoning. It also applies to relationships where people suddenly say things like, "I don't feel in love, therefore I must *not* love this person." And this can be very dangerous as most relationships fall apart because of beliefs like this. Because people think they should feel a particular way if they are indeed in that situation where those feelings "ought to be". Love itself is quite a complex emotion to begin with, so a lot of people sometimes would say things like "Well I feel a little bit disoriented with this person so therefore this person must be very confusing or he is a confused person. My inner self must not like them." This is called emotional reasoning and again, it is a thinking pattern that we engage in without even bothering to look for the evidence to the contrary and this can create beliefs that will cause massive problems....both within you and around you.

Perhaps one of the most important things for any of us to know and understand is that we are all perfect as we are. What this means is that we are all exactly where we are supposed to be, doing what we're supposed to be doing, with exactly the right bodies, mental capabilities, age, sex, financial status etc that we are supposed to have right now to be learning what we need to learn in life. The All in its infinite wisdom has given us the exact tools we need to work through whatever it is that we are here to do. We still will change - in fact we are meant to change, to work through these issues and resolve them - but part of being human on this Earth is learning to accept and work with what we've been given.

The rest of this book focuses on the four areas we most often tackle in this search for our perfect lives. These topics are: health, wealth, love and life. Along with my experiences, I have asked leading experts to share their Meta Secret wisdom and advice and then paired this information with a few exercises and positive affirmations. Use them however you see fit and remember for them to truly work, you must make them your own!

The rules for affirmations are simple. Always use positive statements because the brain cannot conceive of a negative of an object or thought. Try this experiment: Do NOT think of a STOP sign. What are you thinking of now? Your brain creates the object then nullifies it. It seems also that the subconscious only recognizes positive phrases, it doesn't understand words like not, won't, or can't. If you say something like 'I won't gain weight.' your subconscious may literally translate it as 'I gain weight.' Instead you might try a phrase like 'I eat healthy' or 'I limit my calorie intake.'

It's also important to phrase things in the present tense as if they have already happened or exist. If you phrase them for the future 'I will lose weight,' then your goal is always somewhere off in the future, something to be achieved later. Remember we live in the moment, so our goals must be worded for *now*.

Affirmations work whether you believe in them or not because they work with the Law of Attraction. Therefore, if they are repeated many times a day with emotional intensity, certainty and faith they will work quite well. If on the other hand you carelessly say them, then spend the rest of the day self-sabotaging your positive words with negative actions ie: pigging out after weight loss affirmations, the Law of Attraction will attract more weight to you, because that is where your greater emotional focus is placed. It is best to think positive and act in ways that support the goals you want to reach through affirmations.

Positive Affirmations

1. My imagination creates whatever I believe and conceive.
2. I easily and effortlessly achieve my goals.
3. I'm getting better and better every day.
4. I use 100 percent of my mental capacity every day.
5. I am open to the wisdom and knowledge all around me.
6. I make amazing progress towards my goals every day.
7. I only hold on to beliefs that support my goals.
8. I see and feel my goals as already accomplished.
9. I create my own luck every day.
10. I draw positive experiences into my life.

CHAPTER 10

Practicing Wealth

Chapter 10

Practicing Wealth

The Law of Correspondence, the Law of Vibration and the Law of Mentalism, all combine to tell us that everyone has access to abundance. But wealth is arbitrary because it depends on how you see the world and what you value. A farmer with a few acres who provides for himself and does what he loves may be much wealthier than an heiress who has been tasked with taking over a family business she can't stand.

A stream of fish is much more valuable to a starving person than a vault full of gold. In this way all wealth is subjective. Understand this and you understand that there is an ebb and a flow to the world's abundance and your own wealth.

To truly become wealthy, you must become comfortable with who you are, how you interact with the world and the service or the product and value you give the world. By doing this, you participate in the abundance that is all around you at every moment in every time. It is all yours. From the beginning it was all yours, till the end, it will always be yours.

The Meta Secret to wealth is not to try hard or want it too much. You will achieve your desired wealth more quickly if you let go of wanting too much, or focusing and straining too hard to get it. By wanting or 'breaking your back' to get something you are actually experiencing the absence of what you want. Wanting is the same as having a lack of something. By wanting you are drawing lack to yourself. So in a strange way by wanting you are involved in the process of negative manifestation. Wanting is a form of programming yourself negatively to focus on that which you don't have.

Instead, focus on what it will feel like to already have those things you desire. Keep your emotions high on the wealth pole and focus on the positive to draw wealth to you. Act as if that which you desire is already yours. You can do this through positive visualization, using affirmations stating what you 'already' have and erasing any negative thoughts of want as soon as they arise by replacing them with a positive thought.

"The Meta Secret to wealth is knowing exactly what you want and then being willing to pay the price to get it. Most people think that wealth just comes out of having this impression in your mind that you're going to live an abundant life. That's an important piece of it but it's incomplete. If you look at the word 'attraction' the last six letters spell

ACTION. A-C-T-I-O-N.

One of my favorite words is satisfaction. We all want to have satisfaction and again, in Latin' soctis' means enough or enough action. Satisfaction, enough action produces a result.

You know I've been very, very successful with the Chicken Soup for the Soul books. And everyone thinks, oh man you were lucky, you had this great idea.

We used the Law of Attraction. We visualized and we put up posters around our office that simulated Best Seller Lists with our name No. 1. We visualized bookstore windows full of Chicken Soup for the Soul books; all of which came true. But there's a process. First you ask, then you believe that it will happen and finally you must be open to receive what you have asked for.

Those are the three steps that I think of in the Law Of Attraction and the second part of believing is taking action. If you believe that your actions are going to pay off you'll take the action. So, believing doesn't just mean like sitting there going mmm... I believe I can be wealthy. It means doing the things that produce wealth."

"If a person wants to take a quantum leap, rather than incremental steps forward, they have to begin by understanding that they can do that. There's a marvelous little book. It's called 'You Square'. If you square a number you multiply the number by the number don't you? When you square, you multiply your potential by your potential. It's astronomical! I think you just go off the board.

The man that wrote the book, Price Pritchard said, "When you're looking at a quantum leap, it looks utterly ridiculous." But in retrospect, it looks like a natural thing to happen. It was without effort, it was ease and that's what quantum leaps are. What you are really doing is getting rid of limitations in your mind and you're letting your mind just take off and build a great big idea. You start before you're ready; you defy what the masses are controlled by.

You've got to move in to a space all of your own. Understand you're working with an infinite power that's omnipresent. It's with you all the time. It's closer than your breath. Get in harmony with that and just release all thoughts of limitation and make up your mind you're going to take and just compound your effectiveness. That's essentially what I did. I didn't know what I was doing at the time. I didn't understand quantum leap, but I took my income from $4,000 a year to $175,000 in a year and then it went over a million. I had no understanding of what happened. I'd been raised to believe that if you don't have a good formal education that you'd never be able to do what I did. If you don't have experience you can never do what I did. I had 2 months high school and had a bad work record but my income went from $4,000 to over a million.... a year.

Now you can do that and the first step is understanding that you can do it. Quit listening to people tell you you can't. And start to see yourself doing something really big. Write it out on a sheet of paper - the end result. Begin by saying, "I'm so happy and grateful now that I have turned my annual income to a monthly income."

"The Meta Secret to wealth and abundance is doing what you love, following your passion, enjoying your life, being grateful for this moment, realizing that in fact you already have wealth and abundance. You have wealth and abundance to the level that you allow it in your life. Expand your level of openness, deservingness and you can have more wealth and abundance right now."

"If you want to be wealthy on the outside, you first have to become wealthy on the inside; as above, so below, as within so without. First you have become wealthy in your thoughts, then you become wealthy in your outer expression of that. You have to have a wealthy attitude. You have to have a wealthy abundant thought form about who you are and what's possible and when you have that, it will start to manifest outside of you."

"The first thing I want to know is, 'What do you think you're trying to accomplish?' The next thing I want to know is, 'Why are you trying to accomplish it?' The last thing I want to know is, 'If you accomplish it, what do you really think is going to happen in your life?'

Then I work backwards and I look at alternative realities. I say, well, if you didn't accomplish that that way what would happen? A lot of people come to me and they say, 'I want to grow my business.' They'll say, 'I'm doing a million dollars and I really want to do 10 million.' And I'll ask, 'Why?' And they'll say, 'Because I'm making a hundred thousand and if I did ten times, I'd make the million dollars I wanted.' And I say 'Yeah, but you're going to have to reconcile and deal with ten times the overhead, ten times the inventory, ten times the capital, or the money you invested, ten times the employees to manage, ten times the stress. Wouldn't it be easier finding easier ways to make more profit from what you're doing now or from the people you are doing it with?'

The point I'm making is, you have to be able to evaluate the alternatives and the options. I teach a concept that is predicated on taking action and implementing it, called optimization. Optimization is getting the highest and the best use and result and outcome of your time, your efforts, your emotion, your life, your relationships. But you can't begin - and this is where a lot of people really fall down, you can't begin to optimize until you take the time to observe, examine and identify, not all, but the scope of options and alternatives and other possibilities available to you. Number one is to achieve the goal & number two is an alternative goal."

"The most important thing is to quit listening to what everyone else is telling you what to do. Start paying attention to what you want to do.

As a young person myself, I can look back and I can remember going and saying, "Mum, Dad, or to the teacher, I want to do so and so..." And they'd ask "Now how are you going to do that?"

See what they couldn't understand is I didn't know how to do it, but neither does anyone else know how to do the things they want to do when they first think of them. You don't have to know how.

Two young bicycle mechanics from Dayton, Ohio introduced us to a new kingdom. They were the first ones to fly airplanes. The whole world believed that you couldn't do that. Anything heavier than air is attracted towards the center of the world. You can't fly. But they wanted to and so they did!"

"How do you become wealthier? You become more grateful! Studies here in the U.S., show that grateful people earn more money and are better at innovation. So the first step to becoming wealthier is become more grateful. Find the good in your world right now and you'll take a first step to becoming wealthier."

"My Meta Secret about wealth ultimately is you have got to create a lot of value for a lot of people and if you do that, you will bring a lot of wealth back to you. So, by giving service and giving that which helps other people improve their lives, it brings joy to them, brings service and products to them. If you do that, you keep expanding that. Always be thinking about expanding your service to others and if you do that wealth is a foregone conclusion."

Arthur Carmazzi

"I know you've been through tough times. A lot of us have. At one point in my life, I found myself a half a million dollars in debt. I had all sorts of other things happening in my life because of that. But one of the things I discovered was that I was not being true to the person that I really was. I had been focusing on all of the reasons why it was somebody else's fault and why this situation and why that situation and why the economy was bad and it was all everybody else's fault.

It wasn't until I actually started looking at me, at what I was doing and the way that people were reacting to me, that I realized it was up to me. It wasn't until I started looking at the person that I wanted to become and the fact that I wasn't being that person, that I knew I needed to change.

If you really want to make a difference, in your wealth and abundance, if you really want to make a difference in the person that you become, a person that is deserving and capable of achieving great things, you have to look at who you are. What is your identity? What is your ideal self? What are the factors in your environment that can literally bring out the best of who you are and who you need to become to affect those factors?"

As we have learned, wealth can take many forms; wealth of spirit, wealth of health, wealth in friends and happiness and so on. But one of the areas we most associate wealth with is money and business. The following are a few exercises that may come in handy when dealing with wealth in the business arena. Whether you're the boss or the employee, they're sure to help you experience wealth in a whole new way.

No one likes a critic and admittedly it is much easier to criticize than it is to fix a problem. Criticism for criticism's sake to belittle another or make yourself feel good, or to be downright mean or hurtful is never ok. Such criticism means the criticizer has bigger personal issues to address. In such instances, it is best to remember this person is misdirecting their emotions and the issue has very little to do with you personally. However some criticism when it is constructive can be helpful. It can show you where you've made a mistake and point you in a new more positive direction. Either way, here are a few helpful tips for dealing with criticism.

Dealing with Criticism

- Take a mental step back and understand that this is a criticism of what you did, not of who you are.

- Try to understand the critic's point of view, put the shoe on the other foot.

- Separate verbal abuse from criticism.

- If there is abuse, do not tolerate it. Maybe the other person has had a bad day and you have become their scapegoat, or maybe they do have a good intention and just don't have the skills to address the issue in a positive manner. Either way you do not need to stick around for the abuse. Excuse yourself and tell them that you will be willing to discuss the matter at a later time when they are calm and respectful.

- Ask the critic to explain what they wanted you to do instead. If it makes sense to you, learn from it and use it in the future.

- Don't argue; even if you think the criticism is completely wrong.Instead apologize. It is the quickest way to diffuse a situation. You don't have to apologize for something you didn't do, but you can apologize that your actions were misunderstood. "I'm sorry you feel that way." Later when things have calmed down you may want to tell the other person what your intention was and express regret that what you intended did not have the desired effect. And understand this one Truth, that the Meaning of your communication is the response you get.

- Criticism does not make you wrong; it can Jmake you better next time.

GIVING CRITICISM AND MAKING COMPLAINTS

As we already discussed, being a critic just to get a jab in or hurt someone's feelings will only hurt you in the end. But if you want to make a difference and be constructive, use the following tips:

- Be direct. Tell the other person what they did that you did not agree with. Use 'I' language, "I saw this" or "I think that" so you own your point of view. Describe their behaviour. Be as specific as possible; describe what you saw, what you heard and what you felt and tell them what you did not like.

- Don't assume you know the other person's feelings or intentions, for you almost certainly do not.

- Don't give a theory or explanation along with the complaint, as it will distract attention from it.

- Don't attribute qualities to the person that are actually qualities of their behaviour, i.e., if you think what they *did* was stupid, say so, but don't say *they* are stupid.

- Don't blame. Tell them what you would have preferred instead. Again, be specific. People are much more likely to take your complaint seriously if they don't feel personally blamed or threatened. No one wants to be misunderstood or to make a

MATERIALIZING WEALTH

The Meta Secret to materializing wealth is the same as anything else you wish to bring to you through the Law of Attraction. You must first ask, then release it to the universe, then allow yourself to accept it. Bob Proctor mentioned that he likes to use the method of writing out daily that which he wants to manifest in the present tense as if he has already acquired it. A variation of that which I like to use involves making a to-do list of several things which I would like to manifest. Because I'm the type of person who likes everything in balance, when I'm finished, I divide the list in half. Half I agree to do for myself and the other half I give over to the laws of the Universe to bring to me. It is the act of asking, then releasing and allowing it to come to me.

The wonderful thing is if it is done in the right spirit, it doesn't matter whether you believe or not. When I told a sceptical friend about this technique she decided to try it for herself. She was extremely busy and had just moved to a new city, when her car was side-swiped in a parking lot. With the offender gone and the price to fix the dent under her deductible, she resigned to leave it until later when she had more money and could find a reliable auto body repair shop. So she said, 'If this law really works, then the Universe will fix my car for me.' Then she forgot about it and went on with her life. A few weeks later, she got a strange urge to go to a part of town she never visited. The trip seemed inconsequential until she got ready to leave the area. All of a sudden two men in a pick-up truck started motioning for her to pull over. She ignored them at first, but then they started shouting at her.

Worried that something might be seriously wrong with her car, she pulled over in the parking lot and rolled down her window.

The driver of the truck told her that he owned an auto body shop and could fix her dented car door for her - free of charge. Wondering if she was about to get carjacked, she politely declined. The owner of the truck explained that he had all the tools with him and could fix the dent right there in the middle of the parking lot - and my friend didn't even need to get out of the car. She agreed, but kept the car running and the doors locked. In just a few minutes the job was complete. She asked the man why he had helped her. He shrugged, "Word of mouth has always been the best advertisement for my business."

"But why me? What made you flag me down?" my friend continued.

He winked and said, "The Universe told me to." Then he drove off.

As my friend drove home she marveled at her good luck. About half way there she remembered. She had asked the universe to fix her car!

Ask! Release! Allow!

WEALTH AFFIRMATIONS
(SAY TO YOURSELF EVERY DAY)

1. I am a magnet for money.

2. I am now creating wealth for myself and those around me through my ideas, energy and passion.

3. All my investments are profitable.

4. The money I want and need is always available to me.

5. Everything I spend returns to me threefold.

6. My thoughts are transformed into massive financial abundance for me.

7. The more of my wealth that I give away, the more my personal finances multiply.

8. I effortlessly attract all the wealth I need and desire through the power of my intentions.

9. I accept gifts from others with the knowledge that they gratify the giver more than me.

10. I am a gracious giver and receiver.

CHAPTER 11
Energizing Health

Chapter 11

Energizing Health

The Laws of Cause and Effect, of Rhythm and of Polarity come into play when we talk about health. Your body is an amazing symphony. There are miracles unceasingly taking place in every inch of your body. The force that holds it together is something we cannot even begin to understand. Every day your cells are renewing, generating new organ cells all the time. Our bodies are such wonderful systems that they multi-task in highly complex ways to both repair cells and eliminate toxins at the same time! I can't help but wonder sometimes, if you gave that entire symphony a wonderful environment filled with fields of happiness and radiant vitality and joy, how that growing and renewing process might work a little bit better, sort of like happy children on a playground.

A few years ago, I was rushed to the hospital with chest pains. The doctors said I was having a heart attack. It was like a boa constrictor wrapping itself around my chest and squeezing as hard as it could until I could barely breathe. After what seemed an eternity, they got me stabilized and moved me to an observation room. I wasn't out of the woods yet, they wanted to do more tests in the morning. When I was finally left alone in my room, I thought, this couldn't have come at a worse time, the business wasn't doing well, I was having relationship problems, stress was literally consuming my life.

As I looked at my life, all of a sudden it became immediately clear to me what past, present and future were all about. The universal laws of polarity, rhythm, gender, cause and effect were all converging on me and I hadn't been paying attention. The easy part of the Meta Secret is to read about it and intellectually understand how it works, it's quite another thing to consciously implement it on a daily basis - that takes work! So, I thought to myself, if all these laws are converging on me right now, how do I work with them to reverse my situation? Is it possible to just skip over all this stuff and put myself back on track?

So I sat in my hospital bed at 1 a.m. and thought about raising my health pole levels - not just wanting to be healthy again, but what it felt like emotionally and physically to be healthy. Then, I began to think about other areas of my life and what my ideal feeling of well-being was. I thought back to times when I had those feelings of well-being and began to practice feeling those emotions. As I sat there doing this, I felt a presence, something from above came down into my body. It washed over me like a waterfall, slowly filling me up and cleansing me. It felt as if all my veins and arteries from my brain down to my toes were being cleansed. My body began to feel cool and tingly. Somehow, I knew I would be alright.

The next day, I had all the tests. When the results came back, I was perfectly fine. They didn't find anything wrong with me. The doctors couldn't explain it. My results didn't match the condition I'd arrived in just the day before.

The interesting thing to remember about Hermetic Law is that cause does not always have to precede effect, it isn't permanent, we can affect it with our thoughts, because we create our reality through thought. So there is a rhythm to things and a balance, by not accepting something as final, you can change the outcome. But you must do it with a sense of peace and calm. It is something you must believe in 100 percent - don't allow room for doubt.

To me, that was a wake-up call that the Meta Secret isn't something to be learned and put away on a shelf, it must be lived every day in order for me or anyone else to benefit from it.

Meditation has been practiced all over the world for more than 5,000 years. Many people use it to bring a great sense of peace, calm and clarity into their lives. The health benefits are numerous and have been proven to lower blood pressure as well as reduce anxiety, depression and stress. The Dalai Lama has even spoken at the annual meeting of the Society of Neuroscience on the subject. Several scientists from around the U.S. have studied various aspects of meditation and its effects on lamas and monks. Though one might expect meditation to lower brain activity, quite the opposite is true. Monks who underwent CAT scans during meditation were found to have heightened activity in the left prefrontal cortex - the place where the brain registers positive emotions. In other words, it is possible to train our brains to create more well-being in our lives. Mental exercise is just as important for health as physical exercise - probably more so, because we create our worlds with our minds! The following is some great advice from the world's leading experts on creating with the mind…the one tool we all have to aid ourselves in better health.

"Our body is a result of numerous evolutionary changes. It starts with something simple like a microorganism or creatures in the sea. It progresses from small animals to something more complex. We are the final artwork of divine effort. That original blueprint is a combination of different vibrations that are in balance with each other. If the blueprint falls apart due to some factors, we build up stress and become ill in the end."

"The Meta Secret to great health is to feel good now. You do that with good thoughts. You do that with good food. You do that with plenty of sleep. You do that by doing what you love. That's the Meta Secret to great health!"

"The Meta Secret to health is to honor your body. Listen to your body. Are you tired? Are you Hungry? Are you thirsty? Do you need time to play? Have greater health! Honor your body!"

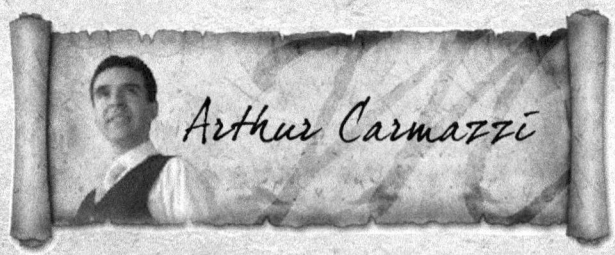

"The Meta Secret to health and having amazing energy, is the ability to know that you are part of a greater purpose and the actions that you take are going to make that happen."

"As you've already seen from Dr. Masaru Emoto, water makes up 85% of our body and the thoughts we think actually create a vibration in the water that has memory. And so you have to think positive thoughts. Again we go back to forgiveness and letting go, thinking positive thoughts, expecting to be healthy, not listening to what people tell you, not taking in others beliefs.

I have been out in the sun my whole life and don't have skin cancer. I don't intend to get skin cancer and when stuff comes on by, I choose not to listen to it. I know that belief would affect me.

I believe that my spiritual connection keeps me healthy. But I don't just believe, I work on the level of the physiology of the body. It makes sense to play at that level. I eat organic food; I drink healthy water that's not contaminated with chlorine and all the stuff, so I filter my water. I eat the right kind of nutrients for my body. I found out what I'm allergic to and eliminated it from my diet! I exercise.

We need a complete system to keep our bodies healthy and then a detoxification. I think its the part that most people don't do enough with. We're taking in so many toxins in the air we breathe. The clothing that comes back from the cleaners, as you know, has all kinds of chemicals in it; just when you put on a suit that's been dry-cleaned. There are 44 known carcinogens in most brands of lipstick. So, there's an amazing amount of stuff that's being absorbed into our body. That's just part of living in a natural world."

"I want you to understand that you have a marvelous mind and you can do anything with it. Don't ever listen to anyone who tells you you can't. You want to start to look at yourself, not as a body or as a name. I'm not Bob Proctor. 'Bob' and 'Proctor' are just two words.

You've never heard anybody phone into work and say "body's not coming today, it's sick." You never hear anyone say "am hand", it's "my hand", "my body, my name." There's something wonderful about you and something wonderful about me and it's the same thing. We have a marvelous mind. We're creative beings and you know that if you'll sit down and decide what you want.

I'm not saying don't be respectful of your parents or your employers or anything like that. I'm saying think of what you want. You might do this in secret just with yourself. This is the Meta Secret. Write out what you want. Write it out in the present tense. If you're a student begin by writing "I'm am so happy and grateful now that I get straight A's." Go ahead, write your report card and don't show it to anybody, then keep reading that report card over and over and over again. Then when you go in to write your exams, be relaxed! Mentally sit there and say "totally relax, totally relax." Talk to your body. You're not a body. You live in a body. Now, this may sound silly because, maybe nobody's ever said this to you before, but go around just repeating maybe a thousand times to yourself, " I'm not a body, I live in a body, I'm not a body, I live in a body, I'm not a body, I live in a body. Then start telling your body to relax!"

"Health is all up here in your head. All I know is right now, I don't have a voice, I don't have much sight. I don't have hearing. My strength is going. However, I haven't been more excited and thankful in my whole life."

"The mind can't be all it is designed to be without the body being everything it was designed to be. But we basically thwart both the body and the mind from achieving greatness. We all have the ability to achieve greatness relative to who or what we are. You can have great relationships, you can have great financial prosperity. But you can't have both if you don't have balance.

You have to respect it. It's trite, but you've got to respect your body. And you have to do it every day and every week. There's a process there too. And the big problem in our society, certainly in Western society, people don't exercise. Ninety percent of the people don't exercise. They don't eat nutritious things. They don't compliment against, to compensate. It's very simple, if you break it down into the little steps like the owl eating an elephant. You'll have the most rich, satisfying, fulfilling, gratifying, liberating life but you've got to balance it!"

"I can't predict what's going to happen to you personally. But I do know that hundreds of people, if not thousands of people have experienced healings and cures by changing their thoughts about what's going on in their bodies.

In my book, 'The Attractor Factor' I talk about a person who had cancer. She experienced the idea of forgiving everybody and everything in her life. And she went through the process of doing that working with a coach. She then went back into the doctors' office. They opened her for surgery and there was no cancer. It was gone! By forgiving everybody in her life, including herself she transformed her body. She reached this place of healing and this place of peace and as a result she experienced a cure."

"It boils down to the question of what vibration is, or what water crystals are. I think crystals are simply information and information is vibration. The pattern of vibrations is in the crystals by various designs. Why do we have the ability to perceive what is beautiful or what is ugly? This is because the universe has designed us in such a manner that all human beings share the same set of values. We are all water!"

"Disease cannot stay in a healthy vibration. It just cannot. And disease cannot be turned into health. But you can release disease and re-create health.

Your body is changing at the rate of millions of cells every second. It's the thought patterns that you hold in your mind that control the vibratory rate of the body. Your brain has an electronic switching station. There's all kinds of material written on thought, on attitude and on health.

If you're suffering from a physical disease, quit talking about it, quit thinking about it. Go to a very competent medical doctor and follow that person's advice. He or she will tell you what to do physically. But at the same time, begin visualizing every molecule of your being in harmony with the Law of Vibration. Repeat an affirmation, "I am so happy and grateful now that every molecule of my being is vibrating in perfect harmony with God's laws. My body is getting healthier and stronger and more vibrant every minute of every day."

Repeat that, treat it like a mantra. Mantra's control the vibration. Get your vibration in harmony with the laws of the universe. Find an affirmation with respect to health and keep repeating it over and over again."

"If you're finding yourself sitting here reading this and you're ill, you've got a chronic condition, you're sick, you need to do a couple of things. Number one, you need to work on your attitude. You need to believe you can get healthy, you need to not believe anyone who tells you you're going to die, or it's terminal or its going to take a long time. Literally we know that we can get rid of disease in minutes. I had a cold once and a person did an exercise with me. My nose dried up, my fever went away, the aching went away in just 5 minutes!

So we know the power of the mind. We know that you have to forgive and release. There is a lot of work now being done on cancer in relationship to resentment.

It's critical to get yourself aligned with Spirit. You are aligned with Spirit thru meditation, through doing the things that bring you joy, thru doing the things that make you feel alive. It could be singing, it could be walking in nature, it could be petting your cat. When you move into that state healing naturally takes place in you.

There's an innate natural healing ability that's always working to heal you if you get you out of the way. By you I mean, your ego mind, your beliefs, your fears, your doubts, all of that stuff. All the resentments you've held that you haven't released. That will keep you sick! So you've got to do some kind of work to get into spiritual alignment and to release the negativity."

"I think one of the most important keys is to recognize in life, that just about all the limitations that we have are self-imposed. To realize that is the greatest breakout.

I talk about staging jailbreaks in your life, breaking out of the mental prisons, getting over the walls of the self-imposed impossibilities. And it is remarkable what happens when you take a look at what really is holding you back. Very often, almost all the time, it's you. It's you! The power lies within you."

"Emotional pain is very real. It's like sorrow, grief. But grief comes in waves. It just sort of overcomes you and then it fades away. You could have experienced some traumatic situation, anything from rape to the loss of a loved one, or being held up or somebody invaded your privacy in some way or another. And it causes deep emotional pain.

What we want to realize is that we are bringing that on ourselves. You may say "Well, wait a minute I'm not bringing that on myself." But you are, by re-living the situation. We've got to separate *ourselves from the incident, from the situation. We've got to realize that it's a very real part of life and attempt to separate ourselves from it and deal with it as best that we can and then let it go . Otherwise we're going to carry it with us and we're going to keep experiencing it over and over and over again."*

As I said earlier in this chapter, the mind is the single best tool we have when it comes to better health and overall well-being. While physical health is extremely important, mental health plays an equally important role. It all goes back to the concept of Ehwaz and balance.

OBSERVE YOUR THINKING

Pick a quiet time of the day, perhaps when you feel you need a natural break. Relax and observe your thinking without trying to stop it, judge it, or change it. This exercise is simple to describe but a little more difficult to carry out.

It sounds passive, but it takes a quality of attention that we are not used to giving. We are used to striving towards doing something.

In this exercise, the goal is to really get to know and understand yourself better. Pay attention to where your thoughts go, how they make you feel and what they might tell you about yourself. Remember all that you need is *already* inside you. When you quiet yourself and your ego - which constantly acts as a critic, you often learn valuable lessons.

Ten minutes is enough to feel the benefit of this exercise.

SELF TALK

Take a moment to check your internal voice. How do you talk to yourself? What do you say to yourself when you have made a mistake or done something wrong?

Do you say, 'I'm stupid'?

Do you say, 'You are stupid'?

Or do you say, 'That was stupid'?

Try each one in turn. What effect do they have? Do you use the same voice tone for each of the three sentences or does your voice tone vary?

'I am stupid' usually feels more immediate – you claim the stupidity as part of yourself.

'You are stupid' puts you at a distance from yourself, perhaps from the stupid part of yourself.

'That was stupid' puts the quality on the action and not on you. It is the most exact of the three sentences and usually feels better than either of the other two.

Remember the Law of Attraction - like attracts like. Therefore, when we speak negatively to ourselves we draw negativity to ourselves. So why would we knowingly bring more negativity on ourselves? Instead, try working with some of the other laws of the Universe; know that what comes around goes around with the Law of Vibration, inch yourself up the emotion pole towards a better feeling with the Law of Polarity, remind yourself that everything happens in its own perfect time with the Law of Gender.

PRESENT PLEASURE, FUTURE PAIN

Every day we make decisions by weighing present satisfaction against future consequences. If they match, so much the better, if not, we may defer the pleasure.

Deciding how much to eat is a perfect example of Present Pleasure, Future Pain. People who regularly overeat stay in the present moment and enjoy the food. They do not cast themselves into the future and consider what they will feel like once they have eaten. They may feel uncomfortable later, but later is too late.

A quick exercise to avoid over-eating, centers on staying in the moment and being very aware of your surroundings. First, never eat as a backdrop to anything. (i.e. devouring a bag of cookies while reading a book or surfing the web.) When you eat, give the food your full attention. Smell it, truly taste it and savor every bite. By simply slowing down, your body has time to register the feelings of contentment. When you appreciate food, the need to have more of it often lessens because the act of appreciation fulfills you.

If for whatever reasons you can't follow these suggestions or they alone are not enough, try staying in the moment long enough to consider how that second piece of chocolate cake is going to make you feel 10 minutes after you have eaten it. Then try balancing the way you feel presently against the uncomfortable feeling you'll have when you're spiraling into a sugar coma, or feel bloated and overstuffed. Some people take the exercise to the next level and even imagine that uncomfortable twinge they know will be waiting for them. Others who are actively trying to lose weight may picture themselves getting fatter and fatter and further from the goal of a special outfit or number on the scale that they are trying to achieve. Then they leave the cake on the plate!

HEALTH AFFIRMATIONS
(SAY TO YOURSELF EVERY DAY)

1. I increase my health, vitality and energy every day.

2. My positive thoughts create the body I desire.

3. I quickly and easily create good health habits.

4. I am more and more attractive every day.

5. I am a lean, mean, fat-burning, muscle-building machine.

6. Divine life now flows through every cell of my body, healing and energizing me.

7. I eat the right foods and drinks to now alkalize and energize my body everyday.

8. I heal and regenerate to my full potential every day.

9. My body is constantly burning fat and creating massive amounts of energy, health and vitality.

10. The more energy I burn, the more energy I create.

Chapter 12
Living Love

CHAPTER 12
Living Love

The Law of Gender, the Law of Vibration and the Law of Rhythm, all figure into relationships. Love is a dynamic. Any relationship is a dynamic. When you are actively relating, that's when the world comes alive, that's when it's fun. When you sit back and start to look at a relationship, it becomes static. You are no longer living in the moment, instead you are viewing it as something to be accessed and studied. When you're relating to your partner or your spouse, amazing things happen. It's dynamic, it's moving, it's alive - that's what all love is supposed to be.

Changes happen all the time. We change. Human beings change. You change. I change. We all change but if you can change together in the same direction, amazing miracles take place. Words, feelings, thoughts are all aligned. And all of a sudden you can take on any problem and it's not an issue. That's what relationships are all about. That's what relating is all about. That's what love is all about.

Earlier, I mentioned being in the moment. As adults we often forget to do this simple thing. We look at time as a commodity. We either feel we don't have enough (I don't know where I'm going to find the time to make dinner) or we've had too much (I feel so old). But any way you dissect it when you peel back the years, months, weeks, days and minutes, we are left with nothing but the present moment.

Children are great at being in the moment. They often become so absorbed in what they are doing, that all time falls away. All that matters is that in the moment they are battling a dragon or walking a tight rope. They are so focused on what they are doing that it seems very real. Not only does it seem real, they have lost their egos and are acting as their true selves, purely enjoying the moment.

When any of us are caught in the moment, our senses are heightened. The next time you visit some place new, you'll notice this. You pay more attention to your surroundings - you're more in the moment because you need to be. You have never been there and so your senses kick into high gear and you have to pay closer attention if you're going to learn what this new place is. You pay more attention to where you're going, so that you won't get lost on your return. You pay more attention to your scenery and surroundings, the smells in the air, the food you eat, the people you encounter. By focusing your attention on the moment, you really begin to experience life. That connection to everyone and everything begins to restore itself.

It's only when you begin to return to your usual surroundings that your brain goes on autopilot and your ego is free to start taking over. When your ego takes over, you start to get wrapped up in all the drama of life. Does it really matter if your neighbor snubbed you in the grocery store? Maybe they just didn't see you. Is it such a huge deal that your husband dressed the kids in mismatched clothes? It's not as if they'll die from the fashion mishap.

When we leave the moment and let our egos take over, we begin to miss out on the magic of life and the relationships that really count. If we stayed in the moment at the grocery store we might have been happy to see that our neighbor was out of the hospital. We might have made the effort to go over and ask if there was anything we could do to help. After all you've been neighbors for a really long time and you really enjoy living next door to that person. And so what if your husband put the kids in mismatched clothes on picture day? At least he's supporting you by trying to help. Besides, school pictures are about capturing a moment in time, mementos to look back on. This makes the experience authentic and makes your kids look more like themselves - the way things really were, not a fantasy of how you would like to remember life. And aren't you glad you have your husband, when so many of your girlfriends struggle to find the right mate?

In both these situations, you caused the issue with your interpretation of the event. You wanted the other person to behave in a certain way and when they didn't, your ego took over and created the problem. The problem wasn't what the other person did. It was how you saw it. They were fine with their actions. You were placing the responsibility of your happiness on how they behaved, instead of taking the responsibility to change the only factor you could - yourself.

This often happens in romantic relationships. In the beginning we are in the heightened state of awareness. Because everything is new, we must stay in the moment to learn about our partner's past, their opinions, likes and dislikes, etc. So, when we are with our partner, we give them our undivided attention. Then, as time goes by, we form a bond with them. When this bond is formed, two things happen.

First, we begin to feel as if that person is an extension of us and so we unconsciously begin to try to control them. We sometimes joke about 'having a well-trained spouse' but in many cases this is a form of control. We begin to place our happiness on the other person doing what we want them to.

Second, as time goes by, we no longer stay in the moment with our significant other. We begin to think we know them so well we no longer give them our full attention. We may talk with our significant others, but we begin to multi-task. We talk on the phone, watch TV, read the paper, work on the computer. Granted there may be times when this is necessary, but if this person truly is your best friend and partner, then you need to make time for them and treat them as something special.

The Meta Secret to all relationships is when we are willing to live in the moment, these two issues disappear. When we are solid in ourselves and feel a healthy connection to another, we will engage in an equal give and take relationship which empowers both parties. Instead of trying to control each other in order to feel powerful, both parties energize each other by actively participating in the moment. When we give the people we love our full attention, wonderful things begin to happen. We reconnect with them in a healthy way. We share in their joys, learn new things about them and naturally grow closer. In this way; though the world is constantly changing, we can change together.

"Relationships are part of what the universe is giving you as a gift. The first and most important relationship is the one with yourself. When you love yourself, you heal yourself. When you love yourself, you become a magnet that people want to hang around and you begin to attract other people and new relationships.

It's all based on love. It's all based on non-judgment. It's all based on total acceptance. The universe has a relationship with you right now and the universe wants to give you more. Are you ready to accept it?"

"Relationships are a two-way street. It's not just about taking and giving and receiving and getting what you want, but it's also about giving.

I like to say that each person should take 100 percent responsibility for the quality of the relationship. If you only take 50-50, whenever it's not working, it's going to be their 50 percent that's not working. So, if you take 100 percent and act as if you are creating everything in the relationship, when it isn't going exactly as you'd like it to, ask 'Hmmm, how am I creating that?'

Take that curiosity and use it as a tool. When you get the answer, maybe it hits you 'Oh, I'm not coming home on time,' 'I'm not listening,' 'I'm not doing this,' then you have the opportunity to change and do the thing that produces the relationship you do want.

A friend of mine wrote a book called 'Making Relationships Work'. And the idea is there is work in making the relationship work. So be willing to do the work. Give as much as you get. The more you give, the more will come back."

"To have a better relationship with anyone in your life, you begin by having a relationship with yourself. Treat yourself the way you would your very dearest friend. Love yourself regardless of all the crazy shenanigans you pull. Believe me, I do this every day! So if you want a better relationship with someone else, love yourself!"

"The concept that "I can't live without you" is a tragic statement to me. The idea that I need somebody else to complete my life, I need somebody else or my life's not worth-while is a very sad statement and I think someone needs to take a good look at themselves when they say that. When you start to think that thought, stop for a second. And realize life is full of stuff and sometimes stuff is potholes and sometimes stuff is bridges are out ahead. Sometimes there's a detour in life. I heard somebody once say that sometimes the most beautiful scenes in life are the ones we observe on a detour. Have you ever gone on a detour and realized that your life wouldn't have been the same if you hadn't taken that twist or that turn in your life? Next time stuff happens take a look, maybe there's something better right around the corner."

"The Meta Secret to relationships is to give the love you would love to receive. The Meta Secret to relationships is to know that the universe is giving you love right now. When you give love to the universe, when you give love to another you will receive love in turn. Love is the essence and nature of relationship."

"When you get angry, look at it. It's ok to be angry, this is a gift. It's your body's way of saying 'I need to release something here.' And in that process, your relationship becomes a school for growth, instead of an exercise in getting someone to please you.

Look at how you can serve them and how you can learn from them as opposed to how you can manipulate them to give you all you need. If you do that you're going to end up with a much better relationship."

"One of the Meta Secrets of Relationships is giving. Take an author and a reader for example. The author is giving everything that he or she has and the reader is profiting from that information from that insight on his or her schedule. They don't have to be in a particular place or tune in at a particular time. They can pick up that book on their schedule and read it to their satisfaction, enjoyment and of course increasing their knowledge."

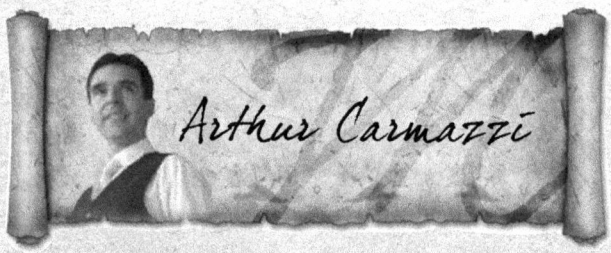

"The Meta Secret of relationships is for you to develop an identity that brings out the best in your partner and to help your partner be the best that they can be in order to bring out the best in you."

"You never find a relationship. You grow a relationship. It begins with you."

Jay Abraham

"Everyone asks me "Jay, how in the world can I have a better, happier, richer - a more joyous relationship?" It's very simple. First thing is you've got to slow down enough and to be externally focused. We teach something in business and it applies to human nature cause business is understanding human nature. It's all about them. The more interested and externally focused you are on the other person the more extraordinary their experience will be and the more naturally they will reciprocate it and recycle it back to you! So that's the first thing. The second - and you're watching me and I've got a serious side and you know that, but you've got to get in touch with your child-like sense of curiosity and innocence.

The third is you've got to be in the here and now and it's so trite and said so often but being in the here and now means connecting deeply and being aware of what people are saying and looking at them and being responsive to their feedback and their mannerisms and the last thing and the easy thing is to again, as I said earlier, enjoy the process. We are so busy, so stressed in our life, trying to get from one thing to another, trying to multi-task. The greatest way to have wonderful relationships is commit, commit not just the time but your being, to being there - to connecting."

"Relationships are about communion, taking our life and making it sacred through connection with another human being. So, communion and making sacred is what a relationship is all about."

"The key to attracting the right relationship is to love yourself first. Relationships are all about love. If you love yourself, you begin to attract loving relationships in your life."

"Life is tremendous!
Love is tremendous!
People are Tremendous!
Relationships are Tremendous!"

"Do you know there are a lot of lonely people around? And if you are lonely I'm going to let you in on a secret. You're always going to be lonely until you become friends with yourself. If you're looking for company outside of yourself, you're looking in the wrong place. You want to go inside and when you get to really look at you, you're going to feel so good about you. You're going to love yourself.

As a little kid you were probably taught "Don't love yourself, that's conceit." I know I was and so were most of the people I know. Loving yourself is not conceit. It's a healthy conscious awareness of who we really are. I'm not talking about an ego trip, I'm talking about really becoming acquainted with yourself. You've got to build a good relationship with you or you're always going to be lonely!"

"When we talk about love we're talking about the greatest word in the world. Leadership is a great word, but no word compares with love because, without love you're dead. There's life in love, there's forgiveness in love. There's thankfulness in love. There's really everything."

Now, the problem is learning where do we start? Because sometimes families have no love and marriages have forgotten how to show love. But, when we quit looking around and we start learning, it begins with me. And when we come to understand we're not through learning ourselves, we really learn the process of love.

You might think you're loving, but unfortunately most people only love the people they like. Love has to be unconditional, that includes loving those you don't like.

Now, in my case when my wife married me, she said she loved me. I told her I loved her. But as soon as we got married and I said 'I love you,' she said 'Well why don't you act like it?' I said, 'I do act like it!' She said, 'You have a funny way of showing it.' I said, 'Well I love you enough to die for you.' She said, 'Try living a little.'

I discovered as loving as I was, I didn't fit her definition. And so, that's why in my case, not your case, no one else's case, in my case I had to discover the love of God, because God loves me just as I am. He made me just as I am, He knows me as I am, He understands me as I am. And so, I said, "God, forgive me, I don't understand religion but I want you to come into my life - and help me." I asked God's help on his terms. Now 58 years I've been learning to be loved and as I am loved, I love!

I don't tell anybody else how they should do it because everybody else has an opinion. But I do know in my case, Love is real. Step by step you must learn - nobody loves you the way you want to be loved, you don't love them in the way they want to be loved. But God loves everybody the way we need to be loved. And then, when we know His love, real love, we love others. But not like we ought to.

Learning to love is a process. We grow into it like little babies grow up. We must learn to be loving and giving!"

Stepping Outside Yourself

Because the Universe is mind, everything we need is within us. However, sometimes the best way to see what we need and move forward is from the outside. While it is a paradox, I have an exercise that should make it a lot easier to understand.

At the time of an event, it is difficult to learn from it in real time, because we are so consumed with the moment, the emotions and perhaps the very real physical danger. Therefore, our attention must be on the basic needs of the moment. However, later we can review and reflect upon the event to learn from it.

I call this process of stepping outside yourself, to review an event with detachment and learn from it, Changing the Internal Movie. A mistake is just that - you 'miss-took' the situation for something else. In true Hollywood style, let's take the situation from the top and make a better movie.

- Start by leaning back and relaxing. You are going to have a private screening of an interesting film which will educate you in the process.

- Think back to the situation you want to learn lessons from. Make sure you are outside it. In other words, see yourself back in that situation without being there again, become a member of the audience - just an observer.

- Observe yourself in that situation. See the whole show in your imagination. You will feel OK about it, because now you are on the outside looking in. If at any time you start to feel old feelings, just imagine yourself stepping outside the situation again as an observer. It's just something you are looking at, not a situation you are in.

- Once you have reviewed the whole movie, stop and ask yourself this question: 'What was I trying to achieve in that situation?'

There are several possibilities:

1. Maybe you were not very sure about what you wanted at the time, in which case it was no wonder you didn't get it.

2. Maybe you knew what you wanted to achieve, but didn't do it very well.

3. Maybe what you wanted then wasn't right for that scenario. You may want to change that now and make it current.

Ask yourself following questions:

- What advice would you give yourself in that situation with the benefit of hindsight?

- What can you learn from that incident so that it will not happen again in exactly the same way?

- What would you like to happen instead?

- What you did at the time didn't work. If it worked in another situation, what was the important difference that kept it from working this time? What important factor was missing?

Now it's time to edit your mental movie. Imagine yourself reliving the incident, only now you are acting quite differently. See how the situation resolves itself in a different way that is better for everyone.

Then blank out your mental screen.

Keep experimenting with different scenarios until you are satisfied with one that feels right for you.

Run your movie at least three times and blank your mental screen after each action replay. The fourth time you run it, step into your picture. Imagine yourself back in the situation. Go through it again in the new way that you have just created. Take your own advice, act differently, sound different in the situation. Is this OK? If not, go back to watching the original movie and seeing what else you can learn and what other advice you can give yourself. When you develop more ideas, step into the situation again and act on that new advice. In effect you are a Hollywood director reworking your shots.

Do this until the situation turns out the way you want it to.

When you use this process, you will get some new thoughts and strategies about how to avoid future mistakes. Of course you can't change the behavior of another person in your mental movie, but it will be very hard for them to react in the same way when you do change. Everything else hasn't worked, so almost any new change should be an improvement!

I have used this process to look at the quarrels I used to have with my son. One of life's worst ironies is to find yourself doing the same things to your children that you hated your parents doing to you. My parents used to nag at me to clean my room and sure enough I found myself doing the same thing to my son.

He insisted that it was his space, and he liked how it looked. (I remember using the same argument, in vain, with *my* parents.) One of the surprises of being a parent is that you find yourself arguing the point of view you strongly opposed when you were a child.

Then, one day I realized two things. First, in some hazy way I was getting even. Why should my children have the luxury of an untidy room when I had not? Second, what I really wanted was to feel better about how his room looked. My goal was for him to be organized. I had confused 'organized' with 'tidy'. I played through my movies of our arguments and found there were many ways in which I could get what I wanted without provoking an argument. So, by changing my mental movies, I 'prepared' myself for possible better responses in a future scenario.

I have also used this mental rehearsal process to learn from a climbing accident, in financial matters and in romantic relationships.

AVOIDING MISUNDERSTANDINGS

When you think you are misunderstood, don't assume there is a right and a wrong way. There are two views. The differences are in the different assumptions and interpretations of what happened.

There are two important skills that help avoid misunderstandings: First you need to make your thinking more visible to others. Always start from your sense of experience. Say something like 'Here is what I saw, heard and felt….' Keep it brief. You are not making excuses or passing the blame, simply making a sensory statement about your experience. Then conclude with: 'So I thought ….because….'

This makes your thinking transparent to the other person, which helps them to understand how you came to your conclusion.

Second, you need to find out about the other person's assumptions. Good questions are:

'What leads you to say or do that?'
'What happened that brought you to that conclusion?'

You may still disagree with the other person, but you will understand the issue, your thinking and their thinking very much better.

APPRECIATION EXERCISE

We get so caught up in the drama of life that we often forget to notice all the good things around us. We're so busy trying to get the kids to soccer practice, make the evening meeting, or get the dog to the vet, that we become frustrated when things aren't going exactly as planned. It's easy to scream at the guy who cuts us off in traffic, to grumble at the grocery store when we feel like the produce isn't as fresh as it should be, or to complain about the weather. As we now know when we get caught up in these little dramas, we lose the wonder and magic of the moment and the beauty of our dearest relationships.

Choose a time - once daily to make out a list of ten things you appreciate about your spouse, partner, best friend, child, or any other important relationship. They can be physical or emotional attributes, but more importantly concentrate on their interactive qualities. 'I am so grateful that my husband made dinner tonight.' 'I really appreciate that my girlfriend always makes time to listen to my problems - no matter what she is doing or how tired she is, she is always there for me.' 'It really got my day off to a great start when my daughter got up on her own without being told.' 'My best friend always makes me laugh.'

Concentrate on one person a week. For seven days focus on what you appreciate about them. It's alright if some of the items stay the same, but see how many new appreciations you can find each time you make out the list. The exercise should take ten minutes or less. The goal is to more positively focus your attention on the good in your relationships. By the end of the week, your relationship with that person will be stronger. You might even share some of the lists with them.

Keep the lists to look back on over time to remind you of your appreciation for the other person. After the initial appreciation list, especially in the case of significant others, you might want to make the exercise into a weekly or bi-monthly ritual.

Relationship Affirmations
(Say to Yourself Every Day)

1. I notice the good all around me.

2. I encourage others to help me because I am willing to help them.

3. I actively listen to what others say without interrupting them.

4. I create synergistic, positive relationships that are fair, honest and healthy.

5. All my facial expressions are pleasant and pleasing to myself and other people.

6. When speaking with others, I look at things through their point of view as well as my own.

7. I truly appreciate my significant other and make an effort to tell him/her.

8. When my significant other speaks, I give them my undivided attention and focus on their interests instead of mine.

9. I treat my significant other the way I wish to be treated.

10. I am attuned to seeing the good in those I love and appreciating their positive actions.

Chapter 13
Finding True Happiness

Chapter 13
Finding True Happiness

The Laws of Correspondence, Vibration, Polarity and Rhythm, come into play when you talk about the meaning of life and happiness. So often we make our happiness dependent on what other people can do for us instead of what we can do for ourselves.

There's a concept they don't teach you in school. It's called 'enough'. Sometimes what is enough for one person, may not be for someone else and we want more. When we want more, we're setting ourselves up for disappointment, because we don't always get what we want.

Sometimes things will go our way, sometimes they won't. We've got to learn to accept this. That's the rhythm and the flow of life. All of life is filled with possibilities and when we see the possibilities, it allows us to see that failures aren't final. Failures are lessons to help us grow.

By making mistakes, we actually learn more. Failures are a way to add to this wonderful fountain of wisdom, that we call "ourselves". And if we don't fail, they say we don't learn anything.

I have a friend who used to work as TV reporter. One day she was taping a story about an elementary school class for the evening news. The children were very excited and as a result they were extremely noisy, making it difficult for my friend to tape the report. Take after take, something kept going wrong, she'd mess up her lines, the kids would shout over her, part of the project they were working on even fell down during one of the takes. Exasperated and a little embarrassed that something she could usually do on a first try was taking so long, my friend called for a break and began to apologize to the teacher. The teacher just laughed and shook her head, 'No need to apologize, this is an important lesson for my class. They need to understand that all the things they see in the movies and on TV really don't happen with one take. And, it's important for them to understand adults make mistakes too. We're so worried about making a good impression that we seldom stop to teach them the really important lessons!"

Happiness doesn't come from always being right. It comes from learning how to do things better, how to please others, how to please yourself, how to be true to yourself and countless other lessons.

Because the first universal law teaches us that the only constant in the Universe is change, finding what makes us happy is a learning process which often changes over time.

So how many times have you failed? I know I have failed a lot. But over the years I have also learned that I am responsible for my own happiness. I learned that there is laughter everywhere and that if I want to participate in the Joy all around me, that laughter has to come from inside me - not from outside. That's the nature of spirit, that's the nature of who we are and it's the Meta Secret to making everything possible.

The lesson is simple and yet difficult for many people to accept and internalize. Last year, Americans spent more than $10 billion on self-help books in an attempt to better themselves and find happiness. Hay House founder, one of the largest producers of self-help material, tries to help people grasp the concept of happiness in this way: 'Happiness is choosing thoughts that make you feel good.

Earlier we discussed the concept of Present Pleasure, Future Pain. This plays a large role in our happiness. Very often when we think about the future, we base our future feelings on what we are feeling in the moment. We as humans have a very difficult time separating this moment from a time some distance in the future. Because of this, it becomes very difficult for us to believe that our feelings might not be the same down the road. Therefore, we often buy or do things based on the moment instead of looking at the long-term picture. This is exactly why we are told not to go grocery shopping when we are hungry. Studies have proven that hungry people buy nearly twice as much as full people!

The lesson here is that what might make us happy in the moment, will not necessarily make us happy for a lifetime. It's alright to indulge once in awhile, but don't bank on any one thing being the end all and be all. Instead, go into the concept of happiness with flexibility. Know that it is a constantly evolving process, be flexible and be willing to adapt.

Interestingly, studies have shown that when humans are in a circumstance which they cannot change, for example when an individual has lost a limb, or someone has died; things that we know beyond a shadow of a doubt cannot be changed; then we learn to live with it - and move on to find new roads to happiness within that knowing. If we believe that change *is* possible or that a situation can be fixed, we tend to focus on that situation and often become frustrated or discontented in our struggle to regain the 'happiness' we believe we once had.

One of the most powerful attributes that most happy people share in common is resilience. Resilient people often gain their strength through well-formed religious or spiritual beliefs, having a generally optimistic attitude, or having strong positive role models. They understand that even the worst situations can be opportunities to learn which, if seen in the right light, can lead to future happiness.

The happiest people are also willing to let go of their anger and forgive. Forgiveness doesn't have to be a purely altruistic exercise and it doesn't have to mean you were wrong. The only rule with forgiveness is that you make a sincere attempt and that it comes from the heart. Forgiveness helps us become less attached to a negative point of view, which could very well bring our forward progress to a grinding halt or paralyze us from moving on. In the short term, anger can help motivate us to action, but if we hold on to it, it just ends up attracting more negativity to us. We will never be able to control the world around us, but universal laws teach us that we can control how we react to the world. By doing that, we take back our role in creating the reality and the Universe we want to live in and take positive steps towards creating our own happiness.

It's important to clear up a misconception about what happiness is and isn't. Being happy or perhaps more precisely being at peace with the world around you isn't the same as the emotional high we equate with happiness. It is not a matter of laughing non-stop, constantly floating on cloud nine, or always having exactly what you want, when you want it. As the Laws of Correspondence and Polarity have taught us, the Universe works in balance.

Therefore, finding true peace and happiness is more like maintaining a state of appreciation for where you are in life and the world around you. It's a feeling of connectedness and being able to see the beauty in everyone and everything. It's the ability to look at the world and the moment and say 'everything is OK'.

If we were all to take this moment and realize 'I'm reasonably well-fed. I'm not too hot or too cold. I'm not too sleepy or too jittery. I'm not in pain. (Even if you are terminal, in this moment you are still here and still alive.) I'm not being yelled at or beaten.' In this very moment of reading this book, you are fine. For the most part, life is a series of these 'being fine' moments. It is how we look at our past and our future that give us the aggravation. When we mix this with the perception of our ego, we begin to feel unrest and unhappiness.

It's also important to understand that everyone has their own internal happiness set point. Some people are naturally more outgoing and fun-loving than others. Happiness, like wealth, is subjective. The good news is no matter whether you're a joyful extrovert who spreads sunshine wherever you go, or more of an introvert who subtly adds a splash of happiness here and there, no matter how bad things get, with time we always return to our preset happiness level.

The true Meta Secret to happiness is that there is no secret. It is a choice that we make. So the best thing you can do for yourself is to learn what makes you happiest. Make a list of happy things and learn how you can bring more of them into your life. As my dearest friends are about to explain in their own unique ways, happiness is exactly what you make it.

"Here's the paradox of being Human. Real happiness is only available in the moment. If you're brooding on the past, or obsessed about the future, even if you're looking forward to something that could be magnificent in the future, it's not quite the same sort of anchored contentment that you get from really being in the moment. And yet, we human beings seem to be perpetually some place else. That's kind of like one definition of the human predicament, the human condition. We are perpetually thinking about the past, the future, something to the right, something to the left, something else. I think the paradox to happiness is you do have to have dreams and aspirations and you have to be anchored, rooted and happy where you are. Not always easy to do but I keep trying."

W. Mitchell

"Happiness is a point of view. Am I Happy? Yea, I think I am. WOW! Isn't that amazing! I think of people who say they are bored. I think how can somebody be bored? Sometimes I wish I could find time to be bored. How can somebody always be sad. Of course we're sad when we lose somebody that we love. Or when the project that we're working on so long doesn't work out. Temporary sadness is a very human condition. How could you be happy? Maybe, by finding things to do that make you happy."

Joe Vitale

"Happiness is what you want and happiness you can have right now! Why aren't you feeling happy? Why isn't anybody feeling happy? Because psychologically they use happiness as a motivator. They think that being unhappy, angry, desperate, frustrated, whatever the feeling might be that is not happiness, that it will whip them forward. It'll make them take action. And it's something that actually shoots themselves in the foot. Because, when you are happy now, which is available to you right now, you know what your choices are. You can see what your decisions are to be and you can more clearly decide on what to do next."

"Do you know, frequently people come and ask me "You know, I'm miserable what can I do?" And I frequently tell them, "Get over it!" You see, if you're miserable, your mind is focused on the past. There's a Meta concept that would take you over any miserable concept in a heartbeat. Focus on right now! See you're miserable because of something that happened that you didn't want to happen. Or something he said, she said or they did. Forget it! It's in the past! And quit worrying about the future! You know, if you just thought about the electrical system in your body it would blow your mind. You'll be so dazzled by yourself. Do you have any idea the number of electrical charges that must fly through your body for the simple object of writing your name? See, your brain is an electronic switching station and you've got one and you can activate brain cells. You're not a brain - you have a brain. And you can activate brain cells and you can set up any vibration you want. If it's a negative vibration you're going to be unhappy. If it's a positive one you're going to be happy! Every brain cell has a positive and a negative pole. Everything that you look at is going to be impregnated in the cells of your brain. Now you're either going to look at the positive or negative side of it. What side do you want to live in? I choose to look at the good side of the situation. Put yourself in a good vibration. Your electrical system, your central nervous system is phenomenal. Think of the blood in your body. Do you know it circulates through hundreds of miles of passageway every thirty-three seconds; carries all the food in and all the garbage out in one sweeping change? If you thought of that for a while you couldn't possibly be miserable. You'd be, you'd just be blown away with yourself. You have got more power in your little

finger than you need to light up your home for a year. There's about 11 million kilowatt hours per pound potential energy wrapped up in your body. And you're probably saying "I haven't got any energy." That's because you are miserable. Get over it! Focus on now! Put a smile on your face!"

"If you want to be happy, come back into this moment and do what you love in this moment."

"Live, Laugh and Love. Shine like the star that you are!"

"Do you know you hear people say they need help handling all the worries, what they really need help with is understanding who they are. You see worry is nothing. It's the outgrowth of ignorance and understanding that is it's polar opposite. Worry and doubt are very closely related. It's a Psychic disease and the cause of it is ignorance!"

"Whatever has happened in your life. Whatever's going on for you. If it's not the way you want it. Any situation, consider the fact that everything happens for a reason. And that reason is there to serve you. How can you reframe this? How can you re-look at this in such a way that helps you. That supports you. That puts you on the path to success and positivity again. It doesn't help you to be negative. It doesn't help you to wallow. All that can do is bring you down. It's time to change your mind! It's time to re-frame, re-look at it, have a new perspective, a new view and put this in the light of 'this was there to serve you'. There are no accidents in the Universe. This happened for a reason. And that reason is there to help you!"

"The Meta Secret to happiness is that there is perfection in imperfection. That when we accept our environment for what it is and the people around us for who they are, we can make a big difference!"

Joe Vitale

You have to realize that the point of power in your life is in this moment. People think about the future and they throw their power into the future. There is no future. When it gets here it is called now! It's called this moment! People think about the past and they throw their power into the past! But there is no past! It's Gone! When you think about the past, you think about it in this moment! This moment is all there is. And you can be happy in this moment. When you are everything is taking care of, all is Well!"

Dan Poynter

"Happiness! What makes you happy? Everyone is not the same. For me, it's research. I love researching and writing and speaking and putting multi-media programs together. And this allows me to do something else that I love- traveling the world! I travel more than six thousand miles - that's 9, 000 kilometers every week! I've been to more than 52 countries, I board an airplane every 2½ days, I've been around the world more than 16 times in just a couple of years. I enjoy that! Meeting new people, meeting new audiences, helping people. What makes you happy? That's what makes me happy!"

"We grow up with the idea rich people are unhappy. Well I know rich people that are laughing. They're very happy. And of course I know people that are very wealthy and are very unhappy. I remember Earl Nightingale saying one time, "Since it doesn't make any difference whether you are rich or not, if you're happy or not, you might as well be wealthy and then if you're miserable well at least then you can be miserable in comfort."

We've got to understand that all the money in the world is available to us. But we have to earn it. Now that does not mean we should work. This is where the Meta Secret really comes into play. Working happens to be the very worst way to earn money. We should work for satisfaction. People should go to work at what they love doing. When we think of work, what we are really talking about is how we spend our days! Work has probably a bad energy attached to it. We should spend our days doing what we absolutely love to do."

"A key component to lift yourself out of depression is Human Connection. Go connect with another human being. Another powerful tool is movement and a third is laughter. Go play and have some fun and watch your spirits begin to lift."

"The Meta Secret of life is to realize that the journey is the thing!"

"When it comes to the fear of failure, you look at your life and you ask, "If I pursue my dream, my passion, my love and it doesn't work out will I still be okay? Can I still love myself? Will life still go on?" When you realize that the answer is YES, you remove the fear of failure. When you remove the fear of failure, you have energy to go forward and actually make it a success. Well what about the fear of success? When you are successful you can make a difference in the world. If you really want the world to be a happy, prosperous place, contribute a happy and prosperous person to it - YOU!"

"Most of us, when we approach happiness, are looking for someone out there to make us happy. Some event to occur and then we'll be happy. If I get to the retirement stage, if I get my car, if my *wife is nice to me, if my son comes home on time, then I'll be happy. The truth is, happiness is an inside job! It's a choice. When I have an expectation on how someone else should be, I've given my power over to them! What I want to do is simply learn how to create joy and happiness inside myself. And we can do that in numerous ways. By doing the things we love, by focusing on the good qualities in ourself, by choosing to focus on the good qualities in others instead of being judgmental. Once we realize that happiness is an inside job and I get to be as happy as I choose to be, not as happy as other people make me, the reality is I can move into the state of pretty much constant joy and bliss."*

"Look you have a mission to do. You have to find meaning in your life and you have to share it with others. There's a whole world out there that is suffering, that is in survival, they are grieving and they are hurting. You and I can make a difference. You begin right now by looking at your life no matter what's going on in your life right now and you find the good in it, the positive in it, the growth-oriented reasons for whatever it happens to be. You find the good in it and whatever's happening you turn it to something positive, you turn it to something good and you go and share it with the world. You will become an inspiration to others. People model other people's behavior and that's how the world changes. You be that inspiration for success! You be the model for change! You be that person that has meaning in their life and you will give meaning to yourself and others. It all begins with you!"

"Stuff happens. Life happens. And then - you get to choose!"

"You have always had. You have at this moment. You will always have in the future the power to achieve, to accomplish, to have anything and everything you want - in terms of monetary wealth, in terms of prosperity, in terms of health, in terms of happiness, relationships. However, it will never ever occur until and unless and until after you first are clear on the specific goals. # 2 you are very clear on the action steps, operative word is action steps, you have to take. # 3 you have an action-step based plan, a strategy and the steps are just the tactics. You implement it in a timely, regular scheduled way. # 4 you monitor, you pause, you are really paying attention to your progress and you adjust it and it's not what you want and you adjust it higher and its better than you want. # 5 you focus on other people's benefit. You don't be self-consumed. You do those 5 things - the world really is your oyster."

"This is our Home! We have nowhere else to go. Earth gives us everything we need to celebrate life. Everything you do will either hurt or heal our planet!"

"Do you know, you find people that are quite comfortable with what's termed uncertainty. The truth is there isn't any uncertainty. There's only the law. And the law decrees that everything happens the way its supposed to happen. If we build the image in our mind of what we want and we're true to that image, that'll control the vibration we're in, that controls what we do and it controls what we attract. Now, the problem is, we let that image get out of the way every now and then and we're controlled by something outside! And that takes us off track. We've got to correct it and come back on track.

Now, people who have no image that's controlling their life - they have no direction, their life is just about as uncertain as anything you've ever seen because they're the plaything for everything that's going on around them. They live like a cork in the ocean or a leaf falling from a tree. They're just blowing everywhere. But if a person that has direction in their life there's no uncertainty! There's only good stuff coming. It's stuff that is going to cause the image in our mind to move into form. And so we wake up everyday wondering what part of it is going to show up today and where's it coming from and who's going to deliver it. Every day holds something really good for us. Alfred Adler, the great psychologist said "I am grateful to the idea that has used me." I love that! Get a Big idea and understand that you're going to see it move into form and that's just as certain as the night following the day because thats governed by law too."

REHEARSING SUCCESS

Have you ever stopped to notice how many times we expect the worst? We brainstorm worst case scenarios, fear the worst, expect the worst, are sure our friends or loved ones will think the worst of us and so on. The sayings about the worst are endless and so society conditions us to prepare for the worst. But what if we were to flip that? Instead of activating the worst by concentrating on it and drawing it to us, what if we were to think the best?

None of us know what will happen in the future, therefore it is just as realistic to prepare for the best in order to make sure that everything goes as smoothly as possible as it would be to prepare for the worst. Realistically, all any of us can ever do is react to the moment as best we can.

So what would preparing for the best look like?

- Catch yourself in the act of preparing for a worst-case scenario and erase it from your mind. Congratulate yourself on catching it and working towards changing your thought pattern. Then replace the old scene with a best-case scenario. Replay the internal scene over and over until the worst-case scenario is a distant memory. The more often you pay attention and correct yourself, the easier best-case scenarios will become.

- You might also try taking a pro-active approach. Instead of waiting for a worst-case thought to sneak up on you, try formulating a best-case on your own. It can be anything from improving your performance in a favorite sport to speaking in front of a live audience. You may begin the process by physically watching a role model and then replaying the scene with you in their place. Replay the scene over and over until you get the feeling of actually having the skill.

Dealing with Worry

We all worry from time to time. It's a very normal and human behaviour, but it also a very fruitless behaviour and instant happiness zapper. It will never make you feel better. It doesn't help anyone. It doesn't stop anything. And it certainly can't fix anything.

So how can you stop it? First, make a list of your top worries. Then identify when you tend to worry most. See if there are any patterns. Is there something in particular that triggers your worry? Does your worry happen in a domino effect with one thing triggering another and then another? Do you hear a little voice in your head - either your own or someone else's? Do you picture vivid scenes and let your imagination run away with you?

Once you have identified your pattern, common links, or triggers, you can set up a strategy to overcome your worries.

Ask yourself how likely the worry is to actually happen. On a scale of one-to-ten what are the odds that this thing will come to fruition? Is it likely enough or important enough to plan for? If it is, what would realistically happen if your worries were realized? For instance, it might make sense to avoid driving your car until you can get new brakes, if you're worried that your car might crash because the brakes are old and wearing out. It wouldn't make sense to avoid driving your car because you're afraid that the perfectly good brakes are going to give out at any moment.

Plan only if there is a real need. Use your imagination to come up with as many ways of correcting the situation as you can. In the case of the car, maybe you'll take the bus until you can get it into the shop. That might help you reduce your carbon footprint and maybe lead to making a new friend on the bus. (Remember, this is planning for the best, as well as solving your worry woes.) Or maybe, you hitch a ride with your cute neighbour and he ends up asking you out on a date. Maybe taking the car into the shop saves you a bundle because the dealership is running a half-off special that day. Maybe you take the car in and the mechanic offers to buy the car from you because he's been trying to rebuild a car just like yours for sentimental reasons and he needs the extra parts. Or maybe you're worried that you're just plain cursed and the car is the final nail in your coffin. But when you take it in, the mechanic tells you, "Your car is in great shape." That piece of news becomes the one thing that not only went right for you today, it put your worry to rest. Preparing for the best can be a great tool to help you strategize for a better situation.

DREAM MAP

Once a year, usually at the beginning of the year, it's nice to make a dream map. The concept is simple. Make a list of all the things you would like to draw to you or accomplish in the coming year. I have a friend who cuts out visual representations from magazines, such as a plate of healthy food for eating better, a bicycle to represent exercising, maybe a snapshot of an exotic location for more travel or relaxation, a picture of people laughing together to represent making more time for family, and so on and she makes a collage on her poster board. Those who are not so artistically inclined may want to write their goals on the poster board. You can also use family photos, or even do this digitally on your computer.

The point is to spend time thinking of what you want to manifest in the coming year and then post the poster board or print out somewhere that you are sure to see it on a daily basis. The act of making the goals concrete and then placing them as a semi-subliminal reminder does wonders to bring those things which you desire into your life. At the end of the year, you will be surprised to look back and see how many of those things have come to fruition. This works hands down better than any New Year's resolution and is a hundred times more effective.

An alternative to the dream map is a directions assessment. Choose several broad areas of your life such as health, work, family and so on and do an assessment of what you enjoy about those areas as well as what you would like to see improve.

The Irish have a tradition in which they always set an empty place at the table during their main meal. This is for the uninvited guest, so that the surprise caller would be made to feel welcome. I like to leave a space in each of my categories for the uninvited guest of a surprise goal - one I didn't predict but that significantly may help me on my path to happiness. Some years, I welcome several.

When you have general goals outlined, start to work on more specific plans. Make sure to state your plans in the positive. Instead of 'I want to lose weight,' try 'I want to feel and look better.' Instead of 'to reach that goal I will diet and cut out all sugars or carbs,' try 'I will explore tasty, healthy alternatives'. Maybe that means joining a healthy cooking class or buying one or two new vegetables or fruits each time you go to the market. By stating things in the positive and making them about gaining something - even in this scenario of losing, we make the goals desirable and worth working towards.

When you have your goals outlined, list under them all the resources you have to help you accomplish them. These can be anything from friends and connections, to personal attributes. See how you can use these things to help you reach your goals.

In the last part of your assessment, look at the things you are not content with in your life. These dissatisfactions will serve as markers throughout the year. Every so often check to see if your dissatisfaction level is going down. By the end of the year, you should be able to see how much success you've had by how much the issues have been reduced.

In either the dream map or assessment exercise it is important to take the time to physically create a representation of your goals, either through artwork, writing or typing. By bringing these goals into representational form your brain begins to shift how these goals are approached. Your subconcious mind begins then to develop Strategies and ways to achieve them and they become more concrete objectives.

HAPPINESS AFFIRMATIONS
(SAY TO YOURSELF EVERY DAY)

1. I constantly create feelings of faith, certainty and confidence within myself.

2. I am happy because I create a happy reality for myself.

3. I appreciate the world around me and view everything that comes to me as a gift that I can learn from.

4. I can find something good in everything and everyone.

5. I am truly grateful for everything I have.

6. I recognize all opportunities for the gifts that they are and pursue them boldly with courage.

7. I am responsible for my own happiness. I have the ability to change anything in my life that I choose to change.

8. My well-being expands with every breath I take.

9. Whatever I imagine is possible.

10. When I quiet myself and open up to my subconscious, I receive wisdom and knowledge for my highest good. I trust that all I need is already inside me.

Chapter 14
The Best Days Of Our Lives

Chapter 14
The Best Days Of Our Lives

It was only April, but already the air was hot and so thick with humidity. The green canopy of the Malaysian jungle spread out below me like a thick emerald carpet, as I stared out the window of the tiny Cessna. I've travelled so often over these last thirty years that the flights all seem to blend together. But this trip was going to be different. It wasn't another business venture.

Anticipation of the event ahead coursed through my veins. The plane dipped to the right and Ehwaz shifted in my pocket. I patted the rune I had carried for so long, as I thought about all I'd learned since my journey began.

The plane began its descent. It wouldn't be long now. As I leaned back in my seat I reflected on the wisdom of the ages that I now taught others.

The Meta Secret lets you know that your life can be exactly what you wish. It gives you the wisdom to keep your moods and energy vibrating at your highest levels and it helps you uncover the tools best suited for your journey through life. With this knowledge you are now aware of how to manifest exactly what you want.

Remember, the first law of the Universe tells us that the process of influencing our environment comes from our mental power. Because the Universe is mental, we have complete control over every aspect of our lives. We must take time to notice our dreams, they often tell us about something we are missing in life. They can provide the clues we need to enrich our experiences. Sometimes, they are the foundation of what we need to manifest our ideal lives. The Universe is mental!

The second law helps us to understand that we are more than just physical beings bound to this time and place. We have come as beings of light to this time and place to learn valuable lessons in a physical form. But it is a multi-faceted experience because we exist on three planes, physical, mental and spiritual. To have a well-balanced, happy life we must nourish all three, like a well-tuned orchestra, all three were made to work in concert with each other.

Everything vibrates. The third law helps us to understand that vibration is necessary to existence. If we let our vibrations sink too low, we become sick or depressed and our body suffers. Love is the way to keep our vibrations up. It comes through appreciation and a sense of gratitude. When we love, we are connected to the world and everything in it. We take on the vibration of the ALL. As we learn these lessons and pass them on to the next generation we raise the vibration of humanity through building a stronger connection to each other and greater understanding of the world.

The Law of Polarity teaches us that everything has an opposite and yet those opposites are really just degrees of the same thing, just waiting to be reconciled. When we understand this, we are better able to work with the people and situations in our lives. By defining these poles we can incrementally work to achieve exactly what we want. This technique works especially well when dealing with emotions. Sadness can give way to happiness, hate to love, pain to pleasure.

When need be, the Law of Rhythm can be neutralized with the Law of Polarity. When you notice the swinging pendulum, you no longer have to be a slave to it. Push your poles to their highest levels. Have patience with yourself and do it in incremental steps if necessary. Remember the longer you hold yourself to negative emotions of thought patterns, the more negativity you will draw to yourself. If all else fails, take faith in the fact that this too shall pass. The Universe is always changing and in time the pendulum will swing in a more positive direction for you.

The Three Initiates phrased it this way: *"To destroy an undesirable rate of mental vibration, put into operation the Principle of Polarity and concentrate upon the opposite pole to that which you desire to suppress. Kill out the undesirable by changing its polarity."*

The Law of Gender can help you to overcome self-doubt and procrastination. Female and male energy always work in balance unless blocked by judgment or negativity - which stem from fear. One of the best ways to experience balanced energy is to engage in giving and receiving daily.

Nothing escapes the Law of Cause and Effect, but we can use the higher laws of the Universe to overcome the lower laws of everyday life. When we use universal law to attract what we want through positive thinking or action; when we raise our vibrational poles and when we become aware of the balance of gender, we are working from a higher plane and will no longer be carried away with the petty dramas of life.

Therefore when you learn how to keep negative thought patterns from looping through your head and learn to fill up with the inner energy of universal laws, you evolve to a higher, calmer and better way of life.

Part of the process involves becoming conscious of the moment. When you are aware of yourself, when you give proper attention to loved ones or the task at hand, life comes into crisper, cleaner focus. Things begin to flow more smoothly and work more easily for you.

Once you achieve this love and connection with the world, nothing and no one can take it away from you. The beautiful thing about this is that true love, real love, the kind that comes from the Universe, the ALL, is never-ending. You can fill up forever and never drain the supply. So no one will ever be able to pull more energy from you than you will be able to replace. The really wonderful thing about this is once you know how to generate your own love the Law of Attraction comes into play. The more you give, the more you get. The only rule is that you can't get sloppy. You must always remain conscious of it and do your part. Remember "From Abundance you take Abundance and still Abundance remains"

Knowing the Meta Secret is not enough. To hoard the Meta Secret is vain and foolish. There is unlimited abundance in the Universe! When you don't use the laws of the Universe you prevent yourself from having the life you want, the life you are destined for, and you prevent others from helping you create that life.

I stepped out of the plane. A landing zone had been cleared, but other than that the jungle grew as wild and untamed as ever.

'This way, Dr. Gill,' encouraged my young guide.

I followed him to the edge of the cliff and peered down into the darkness, into the grotto where my journey had begun so many years before. As I stood there in the moment, the green of the vines intensified, the hum of the jungle turned to music and the perfume of the earth danced in my nose. I sank to the ground, drawn into a connection with this place which had changed my life so dramatically.

My head began to spin as scenes from my life played out in rapid succession. Dual awareness filled my being as I watched multiple scenes at the same time. Tears ran down my face, as I realized everything was as it should be. I had done exactly what I set out to do and the journey had been beyond my wildest dreams.

The being who'd escorted me through the ethereal gardens, when I'd died during my amputation, was exactly right. The glimpse of knowledge I'd learned with her was nothing compared to experiencing it firsthand on my own. The laws of the Universe are never real to any of us until we adapt them and make them our own.

I sat in silence for a very long time that day, appreciating the world around me and the journey I was on. It was spellbinding; breathtaking - to realize how the world comes together perfectly when I allow it - when any of us allow it.

Perhaps that's one of the most difficult lessons we as humans have to learn: when we let go and let the laws work, which they always will! We want so very much to be in control, that we struggle and fight them. We forget to trust in the paradox that, by letting go, we gain the power to truly create the lives we were born to live.

Subconsciously, I began to finger the well-worn stone of Ehwaz. It had been my companion since that day so long ago. Smiling, I took it from its hiding place. If there was one thing my journey had taught me, it was that the Meta Secret was all around me. I just needed to let go and open myself to receiving it.

With one quick motion, I tossed the rune into the grotto. It was a new day. A new chapter in the journey of my life was beginning - one in which I planned to be more open to the laws of the Universe and the possibilities that came with such wonderful knowledge.

What I had experienced was great, but from that day forward, I vowed to live the very best days of my life. May the Meta Secret help you to begin today to live the very best days of your life. Remember that while you seek 'gifts' in life from others...Sometimes YOU are the gift!

"Life's a short trip make it a GOOD one!"

May the Meta Secret help you to begin today to live the very best days of your life.

The Meta Secret Teachers......

 *Bob Proctor* is widely considered one of the greatest speakers in the world on the topic of getting rich. He teaches people how to understand their hidden abilities to Do more, Be more and Have more in EVERY area of life. His teachings are based on Napoleon Hill's Think and Grow Rich, and his delivery is second to none! For more than 40 years, Bob Proctor has focused his entire agenda around helping people create lush lives of prosperity, rewarding relationships and spiritual awareness. As one of the world's most highly regarded speakers on prosperity, he is internationally known for his inspirational and motivational style. Bob Proctor currently travels the globe, teaching thousands of people how to believe in and act upon the greatness of their own minds.

 *Jack Canfield* is best known for his work on the best-selling series of books tiled Chicken Soup for the Soul that had over 124 different titles in 2007 under the series name and has sold over 100 million copies. He is also known for his work as a motivational speaker and was featured in the popular book and DVD of "The Secret". Canfield helps train and motivate individuals, leaders and entrepreneurs to achieve their professional and personal goals. Canfield has also published inspirational and motivational books. The Power of Focus, The Aladdin Factor, and Dare to Win are some of his best selling titles. His recent book, The Success Principles: How to Get From Where You Are to Where You Want to Be, combines his lectures and principles into book format.d act upon the greatness of their own minds.

Dr. Joe Vitale is the President of Hypnotic Marketing Inc., a marketing consulting firm based in Texas. He is the world's first hypnotic writer, he created a home-study course called 'Hypnotic Selling Secrets' – and made $450,000 in 3 days selling it online. He has been called "the Buddha of the Internet" for his combination of spirituality and marketing acumen. His best-selling book, The Greatest Money Making Secret in History and e-book Hypnotic Writing are a few of his outstanding literary achievements. Dr. Vitale is also the author of the bestseller, The Attractor Factor: 5 Easy Steps for Creating Wealth (or anything else) from the Inside Out. It became a #1 bestseller twice, even beating the latest Harry Potter book. Dr. Joe Vitale's marketing methods have made people millionaires!

Dr. Masaru Emoto is an internationally renowned researcher and scientist who has gained worldwide acclaim by showing how water is deeply connected to our individual and collective consciousness. He is the head of the I.H.M. General Research Institute, Inc., the President of I.H.M., Inc., and the chief representative of I.H.M.'s HADO Fellowship, holding seminars and schools throughout the world. In his first book, The Message from Water, Emoto documents his findings of what he calls "the true nature of water" discovered in his study of the effects of human vibrational energy, thoughts, words, ideas and music on the molecular structure of water. He has also published The Hidden Messages in Water, and his work was popularized through the movie, What the Bleep Do We Know!?

 *Jay Abraham* is an internationally recognized business growth strategist and marketing master. Over the past 3 decades, he has been responsible for helping over 10,000 different businesses, in over 400 different industries, produce over $6 Billion dollars in additional sales and revenue resulting in Jay receiving lots of media attention. Jay's strategies can add new life and strategic vision to a company that is struggling, or one that needs to redefine or better distinguish itself in the marketplace. He's spawned an entire generation of marketing consultants and experts who credit him as their primary mentor as a result of his past Protégé and Consultant Training programs. Nearly 2000 websites reference his successful work on the Internet alone.

 *T. Harv Eker* is the author of the bestsellers "Secrets of the Millionaire Mind" and "Mastering the Inner Game of Wealth" which are phenomenons in the publishing industry. Eker is also the founder and president of Peak Potentials Training, one of the fastest growing personal success training companies in North America. Eker has also developed several highly-acclaimed courses such as The Millionaire Mind Intensive, Life Directions, Wizard Training and Train the Trainer. He is also the producer and trainer of the world-famous Enlightened Warrior Training. Having been considered to be one of North America's most exciting presenters, Eker's no holds barred

Dan Poynter is one of the publishing industry's most energetic, experienced and respected leaders. The recipient of the Benjamin Franklin Award from the Publishers Marketing Association, Poynter has produced more than 100 books and revisions so far. Poynter's books sell at a rate of between 10 to 20 thousand copies per year, every year! The Self-Publishing Manual was published because so many publishers wanted to know his secret to selling so many books! Poynter was also given the Irwin Award for best electronic promotion campaign by the Book Publicists of Southern California. His seminars have been featured on CNN, his books pictured in The Wall Street Journal, and his story has been told in U.S. News & World Report.

Eli Davidson Heralded as "The Quantum Leap Queen" Eli Davidson has x-ray vision for seeing opportunities and creatively converting them into bottom line profits. Eli delivers a proven system for turbo charging success into explosive growth. Using the system she teaches landed Davidson on numerous TV shows including The Today Show, Dr. Phil's Decision House and as a featured on ABC, NBC, CBS and FOX. "The new voice of personal growth" Davidson regularly coaches Emmy, Grammy, Golden Globe winners and celebrities Joan and Melissa Rivers on Joan Knows Best. The consistent results of Davidson's trademarked success system is the cover story for Kiplinger's Money Magazine as the best way to invest. Davidson is the undisputed expert of creating quantum leap business growth. Eli started a design firm with $17 and a glue gun and growing it to $1.5 million in sales in four years. Eli Davidson is the author of Funky to Fabulous which is an international best seller. And winner of three prestigious book awards, including Motivational Book of the Year.

Dr Meh Gill is the Writer, Director and Producer of 'The Meta Secret' Movie and author of the book by the same name. Recognized by the 'Business Times' and 'The Sentinel' as one of the Top Asian American Motivational Speakers, he was invited by the Napoleon Hill Foundation to speak as one of the Top 17 Speakers in the World in their Inaugural World Convention. Psychotherapist, Trainer of Master Trainers, Hermetic Philosopher, Motivational Guru, NLP Master Teacher, Personal Development Life Coach, Author or Radio-Show host, the title that probably best describes Dr Gill is 'The Man With A Billion-Dollar Voice'! His seminars and talks, liberally sprinkled with humor, hold his audiences spellbound, whether they be from one of the hundreds of thousands of corporate trainings, public workshops and seminars he has conducted worldwide or an impactful personal coaching session in a remote village. Whether talking to thousands or a few, Dr Gill has the ability to speak as if he is directing his message personally and this appeal has made him immensely popular and much sought after as a Global Keynote speaker and Senior Executive Trainer.

W. Mitchell is an award-winning and international keynote speaker who inspires presidents, prime ministers, CEOs and managers with a message filled with warmth, good humor and wisdom. He captivates audiences while empowering them to take responsibility for life's inevitable challenges and to embrace the power of taking charge and taking action! As an internationally acclaimed mayor, a successful businessman who put thousands of people to work, a congressional nominee from Colorado and a respected environmentalist and conservationist, Mitchell's life clearly illustrates his philosophy- that most limitations are self-imposed. A survivor of a blazing motorcycle accident and a plane crash four years later, Mitchell so convincingly states, "It's not what happens to you. It's what you do about it."

Arthur Carmazzi has been ranked as one of the Global Top 10 most influential Leadership Gurus by Gurus International and specializes in psychological approaches to leadership and corporate culture transformation. As a renowned motivational leadership keynote speaker and trainer in the Asian Region, Carmazzi has advanced Corporate Training with innovative techniques and tools that have been acknowledged by some of the world's greatest organisations. He is also the bestsellling author of the books 'The 6 Dimensions of Top Achievers', 'The Colored Brain Communication Field Manual' and 'Identity Intelligence'. Carmazzi is also the developer of the successful HR profiling tools which have earned him accreditation from the prestigious American Institute of Business Psychology.

Gregory Heart voted One of Asia's Top 10 Coaches is an International Master Coach and Master Trainer. Also known as "Coach Heart", Greg travels the world inspiring, speaking and motivating people to uncover their true mission & joy in life. As a "Quantum Therapist" and Founder of LiveYourDreamsUniversity.com, Greg lives for inspiring & awakening everyone he meets, renewing our collective spirits globally! He is known worldwide for his unique ability to unleash ordinary people's full potential with profound simplicity and by going right to the source. The inevitable results are rapid transformations and extraordinary breakthroughs in all areas of their lives.

Joel Roberts Words like "brilliant", "genius", "master" often get pinned on him, much to his chagrin. T. Harv Eker introduces him as "one of the smartest men I've ever met." At KABC LA (the #1 radio market in the world), in the heart of prime time, he was a broadcaster's broadcaster – an artist of the medium, whose dazzling radio career was cut short by a tragic accident that cost him much of his hearing and frayed his auditory nerves beyond repair. He successfully reinvented himself as a consummate teacher, taking all that he had done intuitively on the air and distilling it into elegantly simple yet powerful communication principles, tools, techniques and models that anyone can learn. Today he teaches and coaches industry leaders, corporate executives and entrepreneurs, and is actively writing a book about his work. Joel's clients have been on Oprah!, The Today Show, CNN, and every major television and radio talk show as well as on the cover of virtually every magazine and newspaper across the country

David Riklan is the president and founder of Self Improvement Online, Inc., the leading provider of self improvement and personal growth information on the Internet. His company, founded in 1998, now maintains four websites on self improvement and natural health. It also publishes nine e-mail newletters which reach an audience of over 950,000 weekly subscribers on the topics of self improvement, natural health, personal growth, relationships, home business, sales skills and brain improvement. David's first book – Self Improvement: The Top 101 Experts Who Help Us Improve Our Lives – has been praised by leading industry experts as the "Encyclopedia of Self Improvement

TO LEARN MORE
PLEASE VISIT:

OUR WEBSITE

www.TheMetaSecret.com

FIND US ON FACEBOOK

www.FaceBook.com/TheMetaSecretOfficial

www.FaceBook.com/DrMelGillOriginal

www.FaceBook.com/DrMelGillOfficial

and

TWITTER

www.twitter.com/TheMetaSecretTV

Learn The Meta Secrets directly from
Dr Mel Gill

LIVE and in-Person!!!

Experience the Magic and Charisma of this Inspirational and Humorful Master Motivator as he delivers his Powerful message that will empower you and take you to great heights whilst smashing through Self-sabotaging barriers that keep you from all the Happiness, Love and Abundance you so richly deserve!

This book is your Passport to attend, for FREE, any of the META SECRET Seminars & Workshops being conducted around the Planet at anytime.

For more information and Global Schedules

Please visit

www.MetaSecretSeminar.com

Lightning Source UK Ltd.
Milton Keynes UK
UKHW02f1918241117
313306UK00008B/921/P